PRAISE FOR

A STAND-UP COMIC SITS DOWN WITH JESUS

I am a firm believer in using every gift and skill we have to get people to consider the claims of Christ. Rich Praytor has a heart for God and a desire to see people know him. His ability to make it fun makes this a unique and special book. I tried to skim it and ended up reading it. I guess that's the point.

Ken Davis
Speaker/comedian

Rich is one of the funniest guys I know. But he's way deeper than just the humor. This book shows him at his best on both counts.

Jerry B. Jenkins
Author of the mega-bestselling Left Behind Series

A Stand-Up Comic Sits Down with Jesus is the funniest and most pointed devotional book I've read in a long time.

Dr. Doug Weiss
Author, speaker and therapist

Who made the rule that devotional books had to be serious? Standing up or sitting down, Rich Praytor is one funny guy. It's great when someone can make you laugh *and* think in the same paragraph. Rich manages to unearth some pretty rich truths that settle into your heart alongside his spoonfuls of comedic sugar.

Anita Renfroe
Comedian and author, *The Purse-Driven Life* and
If It's Not One Thing, It's Your Mother

I've known Rich fo⋯⋯⋯⋯⋯⋯⋯e's written a
devotional book. F⋯⋯⋯⋯⋯⋯⋯about God.
Once I started this⋯⋯⋯⋯⋯⋯

Thor Ramsey
Comedian, featured on *Thou Shalt Laugh*

A STAND-UP COMIC SITS DOWN WITH JESUS

A DEVOTIONAL?

RICH PRAYTOR

Regal

From Gospel Light
Ventura, California, U.S.A.

Published by Regal Books
From Gospel Light
Ventura, California, U.S.A.

Originally published as *A Stand-Up Comic Sits Down With Jesus: 40 Laugh-Provoking Devotionals* (Colorado Springs, CO: Painted Rock Press, 2004). All jokes and quotes are sourced unless the source is unknown. Any omission of credits is unintentional. The publisher requests documentation on future printings.

Library of Congress Cataloging-in-Publication Data
Praytor, Rich.
 A stand up comic sits down with Jesus : a devotional? / Rich Praytor.
  p. cm.
 ISBN 978-0-8307-4473-2 (trade paper)
 1. Christian life. 2. Spiritual life—Christianity. 3. Devotional literature. I. Title.
 BV4501.3.P735 2007
 242—dc22
                                                                        2007015234

1 2 3 4 5 6 7 8 9 10 / 10 09 08 07

Rights for publishing this book in other languages are contracted by Gospel Light Worldwide, the international nonprofit ministry of Gospel Light. For additional information, visit www.gospellightworldwide.org.

Dedicated to my wife, Bridget,
who is second only to Jesus.

CONTENTS

Intermission II

Acknowledgments

Special thanks to

my mom

my dogs, Maui and Duke

the Hardwicks, the Yeagers, the Riefenburgs

Danny and Rochelle Kurimay

Alan Schlines, Justin Sebastinelli

Ron McGehee, Nazareth

Tim Detellis, Ben Yeager

and my mentors, Mike Williams,

Kenn Kington and Ken Davis.

Foreword

My job as "Third Funniest Man in America" has been rather strenuous. I have traveled throughout the country making people laugh, chuckle and occasionally run from the room holding their backside. But on a positive note, I have had the opportunity to work with some of the finest comedians in the country.

Now, these guys are not just your everyday, "Hey, I heard this funny joke last night on TV" kind of guys. These are the creative geniuses who *write* the funny stuff that you hear on TV each night. And none is any better or nicer than Rich Praytor! That is why I'm endorsing this book and why you are going to thoroughly enjoy it.

I have a gift. I am an expert in spotting great stuff. I personally predicted the success of the airplane, indoor plumbing, Microsoft and the Intelligent Clapper. I will soon retire on my earnings from my Krispy Kreme Doughnuts stock! I got out of the Martha Stewart stock a week before the end came. Yep, I can pick a winner! And this Rich Praytor book is one of those winners.

Okay, admittedly his book is not a sporty automobile, but it is a really good read on a cold night when you need a lift in your soul. Think about it. When was the last time a stand-up comedian wrote a book about God? Most of them can't spell, much less have the discipline to formulate an entire chapter of words. So kudos to the Richmiester!

I really wish I had written this book—it's a fresh wave in the sea of same old, same old devotionals you probably grew up with. This book dares to look at the Word from a perspective you always wanted to find but were afraid to look for! But best of all, you will find the heart of Christ mingled in the lines and pages of these delightfully written chapters.

So quit reading this Foreword and turn to chapter 1! Life is short, and you will want to see how this ends before you fall asleep on the couch again.

Mike G. Williams
Author/Comedian
www.christiancomedian.com

HOW TO USE THIS BOOK

If you bought this book, then you're probably thinking, *Oh, this must be a funny book.* Well, think again, sucker. Actually, this book consists of 40 "joke" devotionals. There's a joke, then some thoughts by me and a prayer.

You use a devotional to help you "devote" a set amount of time to something. Here, our goal is to devote about 10 minutes of our day to getting to know God more.

There are several ways to use this book. You can read through each joke and skip the God stuff, at which point you will be smote by an overweight camel. You can read it in the bathroom, which is where most devotional books are read—and depending how much Taco Bell you eat, you might be reading this book several times a day! Or you can set aside a couple of minutes each day to reading a joke and then learning about the true heart of God.

The goal of this book is to lead you to take a step forward in developing a deep relationship with Jesus Christ. A lot of people think they're too busy to have devotional time in their day. Some people don't know what a devotional is. And still others don't know how to get started.

Well, I'll make it easy! Turn to chapter 1. I assure you that before long you will be laughing at the jokes, pondering the deeper thoughts and learning how to pray.

HEALTH

The trouble with jogging is that by the time you realize you're not in shape for it, it's too far to walk back.
FRANKLIN P. JONES

In the hospital, the relatives gathered in the waiting room, where their family member lay gravely ill. Finally, the doctor came in looking tired, somber and a little shaken at what he was about to tell the family.

"I'm afraid I am the bearer of bad news," he said as he surveyed the worried faces. "The only hope left for your loved one at this time is a brain transplant. It's an experimental procedure—and rather risky—and you will have to pay for the new brain and the procedure yourselves out of your own pocket."

The family members sat silent as they absorbed the news. After a length of time, someone asked, "Well, how much does a brain cost?" The doctor quickly responded, "Five thousand dollars for a male brain, and $200 for a female brain."

The moment turned awkward. Men in the room tried not to smile, avoiding eye contact with the women, but some actually smirked. An uncle of the patient, unable to control his curiosity, blurted out the question everyone wanted to ask, "Why is the male brain so much more than the female one?"

The doctor smiled at the man's childish innocence and said to the entire group, "It's just standard pricing procedure. We have to mark down the price of the female brains, because they've been used."

Words to Live By

*Do you not know that your body
is a temple of the Holy Spirit who is in you,
whom you have from God,
and that you are not your own?
For you have been bought with a price:
therefore glorify God in your body.*

1 CORINTHIANS 6:19-20

Just Some Ideas

Keeping your body healthy is important these days. If you keep your body healthy, then your mind is healthy (for the most part). God has given you a body to use while you're on this earth, and it's your responsibility to keep it maintained. Do you smoke? Then quit. Do you drink alcohol? Then stop. Do you eat so much that you feel sick? It's probably not a good idea.

When I was growing up, we played outside constantly. I was only inside the house to eat, sleep or because I was grounded. I rode my bike for miles, played tag with the neighbors, set fire to the—um, I mean, played Hide and Seek until the street lights came on. Now, it seems the neighborhood streets are empty because all the kids are playing video games or are on the Internet.

How active is your lifestyle? Do you routinely eat fast food or just plain eat too much? I encourage you to get out of your seat and head outside. Join a gym or play your favorite sport when you get a chance. Don't wake up one day when you're 70 and wonder why your body is flooded with sickness and the bed is wet. Get healthy now and it will last a lifetime.

Prayer

Dear Lord, help me to get off my behind today
and start to live healthy.
Give me the discipline to start eating healthy
and to avoid cigarettes, alcohol and spoiled tuna.
I commit my body to You for Your glory.
Amen.

WISDOM

*The disadvantage of becoming wise
is that you realize how foolish you've been.*

In the town where I live, there's this guy who is about three sandwiches short of a picnic. One night he and one of the new neighbors stopped in for a bite to eat at the local diner. Turns out the new guy is a beekeeper and has two or three hives at the bottom of his garden.

Somehow we all got to talking about pets, and we're comparing them all. The beekeeper tells us that bees are actually quite smart for insects—they even know when it's time to come home. We were a bit skeptical. But apparently every morning at five he'd go out to the hives and flip the latches to let the bees out. They'd all fly down to the park and wouldn't return until around five sharp that evening when he replaced the latch.

Our friend (the looney) started laughing at this point, and when we asked why he thought this was funny, he said, "'Cause it's baloney! Everybody knows the park gates don't open till 10!"

Words to Live By

*To have a fool for a son brings grief;
there is no joy for the
father of a fool.*

PROVERBS 17:21, *NIV*

Just Some Ideas

There's nothing worse for parents than to have their offspring embarrass them. I know that when I brought shame to the family, my dad was never very pleased.

Once I accidentally put diesel gasoline in a 1955 Chevy Bel Air because I thought regular gas was the same thing. Everyone in the neighborhood made fun of me, which in turn reflected on my parents. I think the embarrassment I caused my dad hurt him more than the fact that I had ruined his engine.

Obviously my screw-up was because of ignorance and not because I was stupid (even though that's not what my dad says). The dictionary defines "stupid" as "tending to make poor decisions or careless mistakes." It's one thing to make a mistake, but to continually make those mistakes is considered, well, stupid.

Is there something in your life that you continually fall short of? If so, why?

God wants us to have a life full of joy, happiness and chocolate. Along with mistakes come guilt and sorrow, which can draw us away from God if we're not careful. Don't let your stupidity get in the way of an intimate relationship with God.

Prayer

Dear Lord, help me not to be stupid today.
Give me wisdom in everything that I do.
If I do make a mistake, please forgive me
and teach me not to do it again.
Amen.

KEEPING A JOURNAL

I never travel without my diary;
one should always have something sensational
to read in the train.
OSCAR WILDE

Cat's Diary, Day 151: My captors continue to torment me with bizarre dangling objects. They eat lavish meals in my presence while I am forced to subsist on dry cereal.

The only thing that keeps me going is the hope of eventual escape—that, and the satisfaction I get from occasionally ruining some piece of their furniture and vomiting on their shoes on a daily basis.

I fear I may be going insane. I find myself gagging on a hairball constantly and can't help but think it feels good. I also have an uncontrollable urge to stick my behind in the air. Yesterday, I ate a houseplant. Tomorrow I think I may eat another.

Words to Live By

"Having eyes, do you not see? And having ears,
do you not hear?
And do you not remember when I broke the five loaves
for the five thousand,
how many baskets full of broken pieces you picked up?"
They said to Him, "Twelve."
"When I broke the seven for the four thousand,

how many baskets full of broken pieces did you pick up?"
And they said to Him, "Seven."
And He was saying to them, "Do you not yet understand?"

MARK 8:18-21

Just Some Ideas

Probably one of the most useful things you can do in your life is to keep a journal, or if you're a girl, a diary. Remember when Moses and his crew wandered the desert for 40 years complaining about the things they didn't have after God had supernaturally rescued them? Why did they complain? It was because they had forgotten all the good things that God had given to them. And there was nowhere to get a café mocha!

Socrates said, "Those who fail to learn from history are doomed to repeat it." That's why it's so important to keep track of your life. You will not only avoid mistakes, but you'll also remember the neat things God has done for you over the years.

I keep a comedy journal of all the shows I do because that way I can keep track of jokes that aren't working. After I'm done crying and wipe the tears away, I jot down the specific joke that didn't work and then next to it I write, "Never, ever, ever, ever, ever, ever use this again."

Just as Joshua built a stone altar next to the Jordan River to remember the miracle that God had performed there, you can create your own "altar," a written testimony of God's faithfulness in your life. Get a journal and start writing! Each year look back on all your struggles and accomplishments. One day you'll see how God has used the neatest things to help you grow in your relationship with Him.

Prayer

*I thank You, Lord, for the things
You've done for me.
I pray that I will always remember them
and that I won't take for granted the
miracles You grant me every day.
Lord, take my life and do with it as You will.
Amen.*

BEING TOO CHURCHY

It gets annoying when all I hear some people saying is "What Would Jesus Do?" and I'm like, "What, for a Klondike bar?"
ARJUNA GREIST

A man walking through the woods stumbled upon a preacher baptizing his flock in the river. The guy proceeded to walk into the water and subsequently bumped into the preacher.

The preacher turned around and asked the man, "Are you ready to find Jesus?"

He answered, "Yes, I am."

So the preacher grabbed him and dunked him in the water. He pulled the guy up and asked loudly, "Brother, have you found Jesus?"

The man, spitting and sputtering, replied, "No, I haven't found Jesus."

The preacher, shocked at the answer, dunked him into the water again for a little longer this time. He again pulled the man out of the water.

And again asked, "Have you found Jesus, my brother?"

The guy again answered, "No, I haven't found Jesus!"

By this time the preacher was at his wits end, but he decided to dunk the man in the water one last time.

The preacher held the man down for about 30 seconds and when the guy began wildly kicking his arms and legs, the preacher hauled him up. The preacher again asked the fellow, "For the love of God, have you found Jesus?"

The guy, staggering in the water, gasped for breath as he wiped his eyes. Then he grabbed at the preacher's shirt and asked, "Are you [gasp] sure [gasp] this is where [gasp] he fell in?!"

Words to Live By

After He called the crowd to Him again,
He began saying to them, "Listen to Me, all of you,
and understand."

Mark 7:14

Just Some Ideas

My mother always hated Jehovah's Witnesses because they would knock on our door and ask her, "Have you found Jesus?"

My mother would say, "I didn't know He was gone" and slam the door in their faces. I know what you're thinking: My mother is a compassionate woman.

Don't you hate it when people talk "churchy"? On Sunday they talk one way and during the week they talk completely different. We've all done it. I'll be hanging out with my friends saying things like, "What's up dawg? Whatch you been up to, homey?" (Yes, I'm trying to talk like a brotha!) Then I see someone from church and change into my "super Christian" voice. "Hello and blessings to you my child in the light of our mighty Savior. What for art thou doing here at 7-Eleven?" And then I fly off into the sky in search of bad guys.

I know a lot of people who don't go to church because they see people who are "fake"—who are trying to *act* Christian because they really *aren't*. It turns non-churchgoers off, because in their minds, they think that joining the local church means they have to be two-faced, too.

I encourage you to be real in your walk with Christ. When you speak to people who don't go to church, be real with them. When you speak to someone at church, be real with that person. You will win more souls to Christ by being real and letting people see you as you really are than by trying to act like a good Christian. Our goal is to impress the Creator, not His creation.

Prayer

Lord, help me to be real in every facet of my life.
But especially, help me to be real with You.
I pray I will be honest with myself and with You.
You know me better than I know myself.
I pray for boldness to be transparent with people
and that I will ever praise You. Amen.

SOLVING PROBLEMS

*The two toughest problems in America today are
how to lose 20 pounds and where to
find a place to park.*

An old woman came into her doctor's office and confessed an embarrassing problem. "I pass gas all the time, Dr. Smith, but it's soundless and has no smell. In fact, since I've been here, I've passed gas no fewer than 20 times. What can I do?"

"Here's a prescription, Mrs. Jones. Take these pills twice a day for seven days and come back and see me in a week."

Next week, an upset Mrs. Jones marched into Dr. Smith's office. "Doctor, I don't know what was in those pills, but the problem is worse! I'm passing gas just as much, but now it smells horrific! What do you have to say for yourself?"

"Calm down, Mrs. Jones," said the doctor soothingly. "Now that we've fixed your sinuses, we'll work on your hearing!"

Words to Live By

*No temptation has seized you
except what is common to man.
And God is faithful;
he will not let you be tempted beyond
what you can bear.
But when you are tempted,*

he will also provide a way out
so that you can stand up under it.

1 CORINTHIANS 10:13, *NIV*

Just Some Ideas

Have you ever had a problem and tried to solve the symptom, not the actual cause of the problem? When I was in high school, I had a lot of acne. Of course, since I was in high school, all my peers had to point out my flaw.

I heard it all: "pizza face," "the red galaxy" and my favorite, "Pus Praytor." (Luckily, I worked out throughout my high school years and was able to give all my tormentors wedgies when I was a senior.) Anyway, I tried all the anti-acne medication I could find but nothing seemed to work.

One day a friend noticed that I was putting Vaseline on my face. She asked, "What are you doing?"

I said, "I put Vaseline on my face to keep it from getting too dry. My mother said to do it."

She replied, "No wonder you've got zits!"

I had been trying to correct the symptoms of my acne, but my friend actually solved the problem. She looked past the external and discovered the root of the issue.

Is there something in your life that you're trying to deal with, but your efforts just don't seem to be addressing the real issue? Are you putting out brush fires when you should actually be stopping the person who is setting them?

I encourage you to confront your problem(s) now so that you can live a more fulfilling life. Don't let your problems get you down—that's what in-laws are for.

Prayer

Father, thank You for Your grace and mercy.
I pray for courage and wisdom
to deal with the issues that are in my life right now.
I pray that I wouldn't waste time
with things that are not important,
but instead concentrate on things that
are life changing.
Show me the path to take and give me
the courage to follow it.
Amen.

SEEKING GOD IN CREATIVE WAYS

Life is trying things to see if they work.
RAY BRADBURY

At the height of the arms race, the Americans and Russians realized that if they continued in the usual manner, they were going to blow up the whole world.

One day they sat down and decided to settle the whole dispute with one dog fight. They'd have six years to breed the best fighting dog in the world, and whichever side's dog won would be entitled to rule the world. The losing side would have to lay down its loyalty to them.

The Russians found the biggest, meanest Pit Bull and Rottweiler in the world and bred them with the biggest, meanest Siberian wolves. They selected only the biggest and strongest puppy from each litter, killed his siblings and gave him all the milk. They used steroids and trainers, and after six years they had come up with the biggest, meanest dog the world had ever seen. Its cage needed steel bars that were four inches thick and nobody could get near it.

When the day came for the fight, the Americans showed up with a strange animal: a nine-foot-long Dachshund. Everyone felt sorry for the Americans because they knew there was no way that this dog could possibly last 10 seconds with the Russian dog.

When the cages were opened up, the Dachshund came out and wrapped itself around the outside of the ring. It had the

Russian dog almost completely surrounded. When the Russian dog leaned over to bite the Dachshund's neck, the Dachshund reached out and consumed the Russian dog in one bite. There was nothing left of the Russian dog.

The Russians came up to the Americans, shaking their heads in disbelief. "We don't understand how this could have happened. We had our best people working for five years with the meanest Rottweiler and Pit Bull in the world and the biggest, meanest Siberian wolves."

"That's nothing," an American replied. "We had our best plastic surgeons working for five years to make an alligator look like a Dachshund."

Words to Live By

If I say, "I will not remember Him, or speak any more in His name," then in my heart it becomes like a burning fire shut up in my bones; and I am weary of holding it in, and I cannot endure it.

JEREMIAH 20:9

Just Some Ideas

Have you ever tried to read the Bible, pray or just spend time with God and it turns out to be, well, boring? Remember when you first decided to follow Christ, how inspired you were? Every morning you would wake up and be "on fire." So now, after the emotion is gone, so is your relationship with God.

Here's something you can try to break out of that slump you're in. Be creative. To be honest, when I sit down, close my eyes and pray, I get sleepy. It happens all the time. It's almost like holy narcolepsy. So I take prayer walks instead. It's nothing weird or out of the ordinary—I enjoy walking and I incorporate my relationship with God into it. As I walk and talk with God, the blood is flowing through my body and my mind is alert. Sometimes it's a short walk and sometimes it's long.

Is there a special place you like to go? Maybe you enjoy the beach or a certain coffee shop. Make it a habit to go there a couple of times a week, and set aside a half-hour just to read and pray. Find a friend who's willing to pray with you, and have a quiet time together.

Don't think praying and studying the Bible need to be boring. Find something you enjoy and incorporate your relationship with God in it. Remember, how you feel on a particular day doesn't reflect how close you are to God. It's the choosing to spend time with Him that matters.

Prayer

I pray for creativity.
I pray that You would give me ideas on how
I can get to know You better.
I pray for discipline in that every day
I would make it a point
to spend time with You.
Teach me how to be intimate with You,
and inspire me to make my time with You the
most important part of my day.
Amen.

BEING KIND

If you love something, set it free.
If it comes back, it's yours.
If it does not come back, hunt it down
and put a leash on it.
Rich Praytor

One day an unemployed mime visits the zoo and attempts to earn some money as a street performer. As soon as he starts to draw a crowd, a zookeeper grabs him and drags him into his office. The zookeeper explains to the mime that the zoo's most popular attraction, an ape, has died suddenly and the keeper fears that attendance at the zoo will fall off. He offers the mime a job to dress up as the ape until they can get another one. The mime accepts.

So the next morning, the mime puts on the ape suit and enters the cage before the crowd comes. He discovers that it's a great job. He can sleep all he wants, play and make fun of people—and he draws bigger crowds than he ever did as a mime. However, eventually the crowds tire of him and he tires of just swinging on tires.

He begins to notice that the people are paying more attention to the tiger in the cage next to his. Not wanting to lose the attention of his audience, he climbs to the top of his cage, crawls across a partition and dangles from the top to the tiger's cage. Of course, this makes the tiger furious, but the crowd loves it.

At the end of the day, the zookeeper comes and gives the mime a raise for being such a good attraction. Well, this goes on for some time, the mime keeps taunting the tiger, the crowds grow larger, and his salary keeps going up.

Then one terrible day when he is dangling over the furious tiger, he slips and falls. The mime is terrified. The tiger gathers itself and prepares to pounce. The mime is so scared that he begins to run round and round the cage with the tiger close behind.

Finally, the mime starts screaming and yelling, "Help, Help me!" but the tiger is quick and pounces. The mime soon finds himself flat on his back looking up at the angry tiger, and the tiger says, "Shut up, you idiot! Do you want to get us both fired?"

Words to Live By

Now the two angels came to Sodom in the evening
as Lot was sitting in the gate of Sodom.
When Lot saw them, he rose to meet them
and bowed down with his face to the ground.
And he said, "Now behold, my lords, please turn aside
into your servant's house,
and spend the night, and wash your feet; then you may
rise early and go on your way."
They said however, "No, but we shall spend the night in the square."
Yet he urged them strongly, so they turned aside
to him and entered his house;
and he prepared a feast for them, and baked
unleavened bread, and they ate.

GENESIS 19:1-3

Just Some Ideas

Have you ever talked to someone without knowing who he or she really was—and then found out later and been blown away? It happened to me!

I was at the world-famous Comedy Store in Hollywood one day. The Comedy Store is the place where every major comedian has started out. Robin Williams, Eddie Murphy and countless other comics have performed there. If you get in good at the Comedy Store, then you're on your way. But to get in, you need to have patience, patience, patience, and know the right people.

Well, one day I was hanging out front chatting with a guy who happened to be sitting there. We talked for a while and had a pleasant conversation about life and random things. He asked me, "Have you ever performed here?"

I said, "No. I'd like to but I don't have the time to sit around hoping to get a chance. I'd rather work on my act than try to get into a certain club."

He said to me, "Well, if you'd like to perform, let me know, I'll get you a spot."

I asked, "Do you work here?"

Then he replied, "Yeah, I'm the general manager."

I was a complete stranger to the general manager but since I was a nice guy, he put me up onstage. Let me tell you, that sort of thing happens all the time. I encourage you—no, I implore you—to treat everyone you meet with kindness and respect. You never know who you might meet and what cool opportunities might be waiting for you.

Still not sold on this kindness concept? Wondering why *you* should put yourself out to be pleasant to strangers? Try this: Because Jesus tells us to treat people well. (And more important, you can get a lot of free stuff!)

Prayer

*I pray, Lord, that I would treat everyone
I meet with kindness and respect.
I pray I wouldn't judge people
by how much money, fame or power they
might or might not have.
Give me a compassionate heart to
serve Your people.
Most of all, let me love You more than
anything or anyone else in my life.
Amen.*

LET'S GET SMART

*There are three kinds of people in this world:
those who can count and those who can't.*

Recently a guy in Paris nearly got away with stealing several paintings from the Louvre. After planning the heist and getting in and out past security, he was well on his way to outrunning the police. But he ended up being captured only five blocks away from the Louvre: His car stalled because he ran out of gasoline.

When asked how he could mastermind such a crime and then make such an incredibly obvious error that landed him jail, he replied, "I had no Monet to buy Degas to make the Van Gogh."

Words to Live By

*Behold, I send you out as sheep in the midst of wolves;
so be wise as serpents and innocent as doves.*

MATTHEW 10:16

Just Some Ideas

I always hear people say that Christians need to be innocent—and not pay attention to what other, "worldly" people are doing. They say, "Don't get involved with those non-Christians—you don't want to hang out with them. They'll bring you down."

People, our job is to hang out with non-Christians. But when we do, we need to be wise to protect ourselves. Our Lord tells us to be "wise as serpents." Snakes are cunning and fast creatures and that's what we need to be (well, don't be sneaking around looking for trouble). We need to have a plan of attack in order to meet our goals.

Dat Phan, my good friend from the reality show *Last Comic Standing*, had a plan to become a nationally known comedian. His plan included a detailed list of what actions he would take to accomplish all of his goals. He dropped out of college, moved to Los Angeles and lived out of his car until he could afford an apartment. In less than two years, he became a nationally known comic. He had a plan and followed it.

Are there individuals in your life who don't know Christ? People in your family? Friends? Pray for them and plan out a strategy to lead them into the Kingdom. It doesn't have to be a big, elaborate James Bond kind of thing (although that would be way cool). Once you've introduced them to our Savior, they'll thank you for having loved them enough to take a leap of faith—and to lead them to the most important Person they'll ever meet.

Prayer

I pray that I would be wise in my relationships
with people who don't know You.
I pray that I would be their friend.
Give me the courage to introduce them to You.
Most of all, I pray for Your grace in my life
and in the lives of the people I care about.
Amen.

WORKING HARD

They say hard work never hurt anybody.
But I figure, why take the chance?
RONALD REAGAN

What Not to Put on Your Application for Employment

NAME: Ron McGehee

DESIRED POSITION: Relaxing with feet on the desk . . . [Laughs]. But seriously, whatever's available. If I were in a position to be choosy, I wouldn't be applying here in the first place.

DESIRED SALARY: $115,000 a year, plus stock options and a Mike Williams-style severance package. If that's not possible, make an offer and we can negotiate.

EDUCATION: I'd like to.

LAST POSITION HELD: Target for middle-management hostility and outrage.

SALARY: A lot less than I'm worth.

MOST NOTABLE ACHIEVEMENT: My incredible collection of stolen pencils and copy paper.

REASON FOR LEAVING: Too tired.

HOURS AVAILABLE TO WORK: Any.

PREFERRED HOURS: 1:30-3:30 P.M., Monday, Tuesday and Thursday.

DO YOU HAVE ANY SPECIAL SKILLS? I can eat 5 hamburgers in 10 minutes.

MAY WE CONTACT YOUR CURRENT EMPLOYER?
I'd rather you not.
DO YOU HAVE ANY PHYSICAL CONDITIONS THAT WOULD PROHIBIT YOU FROM LIFTING UP TO 50 LBS.?
My pride.
DO YOU HAVE A CAR? I think the more appropriate question here would be, "Do you have a car that runs?"
HAVE YOU RECEIVED ANY SPECIAL AWARDS OR RECOGNITION? I may already be a winner of the 7-UP $1 million sweepstakes.
DO YOU SMOKE? Only when I'm upset.
WHAT WOULD YOU LIKE TO BE DOING IN FIVE YEARS? Living in Bali with a fabulously wealthy supermodel who thinks I'm the greatest thing since cookies. Actually, I'd like to be doing that now.

Words to Live By

Poor is he who works with a negligent hand,
but the hand of the diligent makes rich.

PROVERBS 10:4

Just Some Ideas

Everyone knows someone who is lazy. If you don't know that person, then it's you!

When I first moved to California, I had a roommate who wanted to be an actor. He was an incredible magician and a very, very funny guy. He had all the potential to be successful in the business, but he hated to work. He literally sat in the apartment all day waiting for his agent to call, thinking fame and fortune would just come his way. (I think he started to believe that whole magic thing!) For over a year, day after day, my roommate sat on the couch complaining that his agent never got him an audition. Needless to say, he had to go back home to live with his parents because he refused to go out and get a job on his own.

As Christians, our greatest witness to nonbelievers is how we live our lives. If people see a "Christian" being lazy at work, then they're going to assume all Christians are lazy. If a "Christian" is known for being a gossip, then people will assume all Christians are gossips. If a "Christian" likes the Lakers, then people will assume that all Christians are drug dealers. I know, I know, it's not fair but that's reality.

One of the best ways to witness for Christ is to work hard every day. Whether you're at a job, at home with the family or just spending time with friends, I encourage you to be a servant in every aspect of your life. By doing this, I guarantee you'll make Jesus more famous, in a good way!

Prayer

God, I pray that I would work hard in everything I do.
I pray that I would be diligent in my job, at church
and in my relationships with my family and friends.
I pray that I would be a good witness for You
and have the courage to live my life
the way You want me to.
Amen.

PRAYER

If you talk to God, it's called prayer.
If God talks to you, it's called schizophrenia.
THOMAS SZASZ

A man was out hunting one day. He just happened to be hunting bears. As he trudged through the forest looking for the huge animal, he came upon a large and steep hill. Thinking that perhaps there would be a bear on the other side of the hill, he climbed up the incline and, just as he was pulling himself up over the last outcropping of rocks, a huge bear met him nose to nose.

The bear roared fiercely. The man was so scared that he lost his balance and fell down the hill, with the bear following not far behind. As he tumbled down the hill, the man lost his gun. When he finally reached the bottom, he found that he had a broken leg.

Escape was impossible and so the man, who had never been particularly religious (in fact, this just happened to be a Sunday morning), prayed, "God, if you will make this bear a Christian, I will be happy with whatever lot you give me for the rest of my life."

The bear was no more than three feet away from the man when it stopped dead in its tracks, looked up to the heavens, and then fell to its knees and prayed in a loud voice, "O Lord, bless this food that I am about to receive."

Words to Live By

But you, when you pray, go into your inner room,
close your door and pray to your Father who is in secret,
and your Father who sees what is done in secret will reward you.
And when you are praying, do not use meaningless
repetition as the Gentiles do,
for they suppose that they will be heard for their many words.
So do not be like them; for your Father knows what
you need before you ask Him.

MATTHEW 6:6-8

Just Some Ideas

There is incredible power in prayer. Believe me when I tell
you this.

I read an article in *Reader's Digest* about a study involving
two groups of patients, each group consisting of a 100 patients
suffering from the same illness. The study group leader gave the
names of the people in the first group to a local church, asking
church members to pray for those patients for a period of three
months.

Nothing was done for the patients in the second group.

At the end of the three-month period, 80 percent of the people in the first group had "great improvement" in their health.
In the second group only 10 percent reported being greatly
improved.

A lot of people (including me) tend to forget the importance
of prayer. We get so worried and frustrated about a problem
we're having and don't even think about asking God for help.
Or sometimes we get upset when we don't get the things we pray

for. It's funny how selfish we all can be.

How active is your prayer life? Is it daily? Monthly? Only when you want something? Just before a meal so that you can feel spiritual?

Here's a neat little thing you can do to get back into prayer: Set aside five minutes a day to pray. That's right, only five. Believe me, five minutes can be a long time. Sit down, close your eyes and just begin to talk to God about stuff. Pray for your friends, family and anything else that comes to mind. Thank Him for the things He's done for you. Ask for the things you need.

I can assure you that if you do this on a consistent basis, your life will start to change. So what are you waiting for? Set aside those five minutes *today*!

Prayer

Jesus, I pray that I would take steps to
get to know You better.
I pray for discipline that I would spend time in prayer
each and every day.
I pray that I would develop prayer habits
and look to You for the things I need and want.
Thank You, Jesus, for loving me.
Amen.

FRIENDSHIP

*A friend is someone who knows the song in your heart
and can sing it back to you when you have forgotten the words.*

There was once a man named Bubba who knew *everyone* in the whole world! Once when Bubba got a new job, Bubba says to his new boss, "Boss, I know everyone in the whole world!" His boss doesn't believe him, so he says, "No, you do not know everyone in the whole world"; but Bubba says, "Yes, I do!" So Bubba's boss says, "Well, prove it!" Then Bubba says, "Pick someone—I guarantee I know him!"

Well, Bubba's boss thinks for a minute and then comes up with a name. "Brad Pitt! I bet you don't know Brad Pitt!" Bubba says, "Brad Pitt! Brad and I were in Boy Scouts together when we were kids!" But Bubba's boss replies, "No, you weren't!" Then Bubba says, "Yes, we were!"

So they fly to Hollywood and drive up to Brad Pitt's house. Bubba knocks on the door and Brad Pitt answers and Bubba goes, "Brad!" and Brad goes, "Bubba!" They hug and catch up for 30 minutes, and Bubba's boss can't believe it. But then he thinks, *Well that could happen, it's just one person!* So he tells Bubba and Bubba says, "Okay, pick somebody else!"

This time Bubba's boss has someone in mind! "The president, George Bush! You don't know George Bush!" But Bubba says, "Oh, yes, I do! George and I were on debate team together in college!" Bubba's boss says, "No, you weren't!" and Bubba says "Yes, we were!"

So they fly to Washington and they catch up with the president at a press conference. They work their way through the crowd until Bubba gets close enough to catch Bush's eye and waves "George!" and the president waves "Bubba!" After the press conference, they hug and catch up for 30 minutes and Bubba's boss is stunned—he can't believe it. But then he thinks, *Well, that's just two people in one country—that doesn't mean he knows everyone in the whole world!* So he tells Bubba and Bubba says, "Okay, pick someone from outside the United States, a global figure—I guarantee I know him!"

And Bubba's boss knows just who to pick! So he says, "The Pope! You do not know the Pope!" and Bubba says "The Pope! The Pope *baptized* me!" Bubba's boss says "No, he didn't!" and Bubba says "Yes, he did!"

So they fly to Rome where the Pope is saying Mass in front of hundreds of thousands of people. They work their way through the crowd—without much luck—so Bubba says, "Boss, we're never gonna get there together through all these people, so I tell you what: I'll work my way up there and when I do, I'll give you a sign that shows you I know the Pope!" and he leaves. Well, Bubba's boss waits and waits and waits and just when he's about to give up, he sees the Pope come out onto the balcony—and right there beside him is Bubba!

Shortly afterward, Bubba's boss passes out.

Bubba comes back and finds his boss passed out and he fans him and says "Boss! Boss! Wake up!" When his boss comes to, he asks, "Boss, what happened?"

Bubba's boss looks at Bubba and says, "Okay, I can see Brad Pitt. I can see George Bush—heck, I can even take the Pope! But when somebody standing next to me asks, 'Who's that up there with Bubba?' that's a little more than I can take!"

Words to Live By

And they came, bringing to him a paralytic carried by four men.
Being unable to get to Him because of the crowd, they
removed the roof above Him;
and when they had dug an opening, they let down the pallet
on which the paralytic lay.
And Jesus seeing their faith said to the paralytic,
"Son, your sins are forgiven."

MARK 2:3-5

Just Some Ideas

Apart from God and family, friends should be the most important people in your life.

When I was 19, I was completely in love with this girl (well, really infatuated). One day I found out she had been cheating on me the entire time we were going out. I was completely crushed. I called my buddy Ben and he came over and just sat with me for a couple of hours, telling me that I was better off without her. Plus he made some really mean jokes about her that were super funny at the time.

In your walk with Jesus, you'll discover how important friends can be in your life. There's no better feeling (well, expect maybe eating chocolate) than being able to call on friends you know you love to hang out with. Think of the fondest memories you have. If they don't involve your family, then they were great times you shared with your friends. Friends can and will make all the difference in the world.

Are you a good friend? Do you put forth effort in the friendships you have with people? If you do, that's great. Keep it up. If not, then go out and be a good friend to everyone you meet.

Commit random acts of kindness! Buy your friends lunch one day. Stop by and bring them a gift (or if you're a guy, slap them on the behind!).

Remember your friends, and they will always remember you.

Prayer

I pray that I would be a great friend to
all the people I know.
I pray that You will help me to serve them
as well as I can
and to always be available when they need me.
I ask that You would give me the grace to forgive
them when they hurt me
and that they would do the same for me.
Thank You, Jesus, for my friends
and thank You for having me as Your friend.
Amen.

TRIALS

It always looks darkest just before it gets totally black.
CHARLIE BROWN

A CEO throwing a party takes his executives on a tour of his great mansion. In the back of the property, the CEO has the largest swimming pool any of them has ever seen.

The huge pool, however, is filled with hungry crocodiles. The CEO says to his executives, "I think an executive should be measured by courage. Courage is what made me CEO. So this is my challenge to each of you: If anyone has enough courage to dive into the pool, swim through those crocodiles and make it to the other side, I will give that person anything he or she desires: my job, my money, my house—anything!"

Everyone laughs at the outrageous offer and proceeds to follow the CEO on the tour of the estate. Suddenly, they hear a loud splash. Everyone turns around and sees the CFO (Chief Financial Officer) in the pool, swimming for his dear life. He dodges the crocodiles left and right and makes it to the edge of the pool with seconds to spare. He pulls himself out just as a huge alligator snaps at his shoes.

The flabbergasted CEO approaches the CFO and says, "You are amazing. I've never seen anything like it in my life. You are brave beyond measure and anything I own is yours. Tell me what I can do for you."

The CFO, panting for breath, looks up and says, "You can tell me who the heck pushed me in the pool!"

Words to Live By

Count it all joy, my brethren, when you encounter various trials,
knowing that the testing of your faith produces endurance.
And let endurance have its perfect result,
so that you may be perfect and complete, lacking in nothing.

JAMES 1:2-4

Just Some Ideas

Have you ever heard the phrase, "What doesn't kill you makes you stronger"? Other people usually say this to me after I've gone through a tough situation. Their comment makes me want to punch them in the throat. But they're right, trials do make you stronger—and they're great for building character.

I once performed at a retirement home where I was supposed to do 30 minutes of stand-up comedy. I did my act for 25 minutes and got one laugh. Yes, only one stinkin' laugh! Those people did not find me funny at all. One lady even yelled out, "Get a day job!" I was not amused. Here I was killing myself for them and all those Metamucil-drinking people could do was insult me. But you know what, it made me stronger. It taught me how to deal with unfair situations and make fun of old people when they're not looking.

How do you deal with trials? Do you get depressed? Are you challenged by them? Do you run away from them? I encourage you to face them head on. Ask God for help as you face your trials, and He will provide a way out. Build up your character now so that big trials won't seem like a huge deal in the future. (And if they still do, then you can always make fun of old people.)

Prayer

Lord, I pray for courage to handle the trials I face every day.
I pray for a joyous attitude when dealing with them.
I pray I would deal with them wholeheartedly
and learn as much as I can from them.
I know that You allow trials to come into my life
to teach me how to be a better person and Christian.
Thank You, God, for trials and help me to
use them for Your glory.
Amen.

WORSHIP

*That which dominates our imaginations and our thoughts
will determine our lives and our character.
Therefore, it behooves us to be careful what we worship,
for what we are worshiping, we are becoming.*
RALPH WALDO EMERSON

A tourist in Vienna is going through a graveyard and all of the sudden he hears music. No one is around, so he starts searching for the source. He finally locates the origin and finds it is coming from a grave with a headstone that reads: "Ludwig van Beethoven, 1770-1827."

Then he realizes that the music is the famous Ninth Symphony and it is being played backward! Puzzled, he leaves the graveyard and persuades a friend to return with him. By the time they arrive back at the grave, the music has changed. This time it is the Seventh Symphony, but like the previous piece, it is being played backward. Curious, the men agree to consult a music scholar.

When they return with the expert, the Fifth Symphony is playing, again backward. The expert notices that the symphonies are being played in the reverse order in which they were composed: the Ninth, then the Seventh, then the Fifth.

By the next day, the word has spread and a throng has gathered around the grave. They are all listening to the Second Symphony being played backward. Just then, the graveyard's caretaker ambles up to the group. Someone in the crowd asks him if he has an explanation for the music.

"Don't you get it?" the caretaker asks incredulously. "He's decomposing!"

Words to Live By

When all the Israelites saw the fire coming down
and the glory of the LORD above the temple,
they knelt on the pavement with their faces to the ground,
and they worshiped and gave thanks to the LORD, saying,
"He is good; his love endures forever."

2 CHRONICLES 7:3, *NIV*

Just Some Ideas

What does it mean to worship God? For some it means to sing songs. For others it means giving food to the poor. Worship can be anything that gives glory to God.

When I was 16, I was competitive in BMX freestyle riding. I would come home from school every day and practice for hours on end. There was nothing more important in my life than my sport. I worshiped it. But after my decision to follow Christ, I realized that I needed to worship Him and nothing else. Once I did that, life came into focus.

I think one of the most effective ways to worship God is to find a quiet place and sing to God. Music is so powerful—I mean, think about it. Our culture is molded by music—the things you see on MTV dictate not only what songs will be hits but also what the popular fashions will be. So we learn something about the power of music from popular culture.

We can use worship music to glorify our amazing Creator and to seek intimacy with Him. Just as David sat in the field tending his sheep and singing songs with his harp, you can worship the same God in the same way. You can sing your own songs to Him. Invite Him to be present with you. Let Him hold you. Then let Him sing over you (see Zephaniah 3:17).

Prayer

I worship You, my Lord.
Thank You for the things You've given me and will
give me throughout my life.
I pray that I would continue to worship You in
every aspect of my life.
I glorify Your name and lift it high.
You are my savior and I will ever worship You in song.
Amen.

GETTING ALONG

I hate it when people say, "It's always the last place you looked."
Of course it is. Why would you keep looking after you've found it?"
BILLY CONNOLLY

A man, his wife and his ever-nagging mother-in-law went on vacation to Jerusalem. While they were there, the mother-in-law passed away.

The undertaker told the husband, "You can have her shipped home for $5,000, or you can bury her here in the Holy Land for $150." The man thought about it and told him he would just have her shipped home.

The undertaker asked, "Why would you spend $5,000 to ship your mother-in-law home when it would be wonderful to be buried here and it would only cost you $150?"

The man replied, "Long ago a man died here, was buried here and three days later rose from the dead. I just can't take that chance."

Words to Live By

Now a man came up to Jesus and asked, "Teacher, what good thing must I do to get eternal life? . . ." Jesus replied, "Do not murder, do not commit adultery, do not steal, do not give false testimony, honor your father and mother," and "love your neighbor as yourself."

MATTHEW 19:16,18-19

Just Some Ideas

Do you know someone who you just can't stand? Maybe it's a neighbor. A family member. Someone who just cut you off on the freeway.

Annoying people are everywhere. As Christians, we're told to treat people with kindness and respect. But how do you do that when you're running late and the guy at the coffee shop won't shut up about his poodle? I know each and every day we all go through some annoying experience that, by the grace of God, we make it through without causing any casualties.

So what can we do on a daily basis to better deal with someone whom we might not want to spend Christmas with? We need to understand that no matter who the person is, he or she is one of God's children. As hard as it might be to grasp, God has a plan for that individual's life, just as He has a plan for ours as well. Maybe that plan includes bumping into that person on a consistent basis. We must always be open to what or who God has for us.

More important, we need to treat that person just as Jesus would treat him or her. After all, who are we to treat someone differently just because we have our own ideas about him or her? Jesus didn't call us only to love our neighbor but also to give him or her more than what we normally would give. Once we figure out it's not all about us, that's when we'll have more than we could have ever hoped for.

Prayer:

Father in heaven, thank You for everything You've given me today. I pray I would be considerate and understanding to people I don't get along with. Give me the grace to be a friend to them and to point them toward You.

LAUGHTER: A GIFT FROM GOD

It's only been in the last couple of years that churches have been open to having a comedian perform in their building. Can you blame them, though? When you turn on the TV, every comedian is cussing or trying to "express himself" by talking about things his mother would not be proud of.

There is a new breed of comedy that is becoming more popular: comedy that the entire family can enjoy. Not only are churches more open to comedy because they know it will be clean and uplifting, but TV shows and movies are also getting cleaner. Corporations want clean comedians to entertain them, not some famous guy they know will offend them. Dirty is out and clean is in.

Because God is a God of opportunity and creativity, He created humor to heal and change lives, not to put down or degrade people. Humor can be effective in teaching God's Word and in breaking down the walls of stereotypes that often prevent people from becoming part of a church. Humor can bring someone back to a church if that person knows he or she will laugh and have fun. (In fact, humor and wedgies are the backbone of effective youth ministry!)

At almost every show where I perform, someone will introduce me with the following phrase: "Laughter is good medicine" or "A merry heart does good [for] the soul." I've been hearing these one-liners ever since I got into comedy. I knew it was biblical and I thought I believed it, but I never took it seriously until recently.

I've often heard that laughter heals the hurting. I thought that was a cool saying and used to throw it into conversation when I was feeling spiritual about what I was doing. But I don't think I really believed it. Sure, I've seen people get healed in my church and in the Steve Martin movie *Leap of Faith*, but I never thought I would ever be a part of something so dramatic.

* * *

It's January 2004 and I'm on my way San Antonio, Texas, for a youth event. I'm not happy because it's early, my flight is delayed and I'm sitting next to a guy who clearly has not showered in the last 60 days. Here's the thing about being a comedian: You can never call in sick or postpone a show just because you're "not in the mood." If you're projectile vomiting and an alien is coming out of your belly button, you've still got to perform. There is no "I don't feel like performing today." You make it happen, no matter what the cost.

So I'm having a "I don't feel like being funny" day, and I've got to perform in front of 500 hormonal high school kids in a couple of hours. I get to the church and they tell me they just want straight comedy, no message or anything spiritual. I'm like, "Fine, less work for me." I'm sitting in the green room (the kindergarten room with the really small chairs I can only fit one cheek on), just daydreaming about not being there.

I go up and perform for the 30 minutes I was asked to do, get off stage and go back to my luxurious, small-chair green room. I hear them dismissing everyone, so I start looking for the youth pastor to thank him for having me there. It has been easy work and even though I'm having a *blah* day, I'm still enjoying the fact that I'm a comedian.

As I'm looking for the pastor, a lady stops me and says, "Thank you."

I tell her, "You're welcome. The kids were a great audience."

She replies, "No, I wanted to thank you for making me laugh. I haven't laughed in three months."

"Why?"

"My daughter was killed in a car accident and nothing in my life has been worth smiling about. Today was the first time I've laughed in three months. Today God said to me it's okay to move on with my life. Thank you for making me laugh."

Laughter can heal a broken heart.

* * *

Comedy can not only heal emotional hurt but physical limitations as well. And I have been lucky enough to see firsthand what God can do through humor.

I was working with Kenn Kington and Mike Williams, two phenomenal comedians that I've looked up to since my career started, doing an Ultimate Comedy Theater event at Woodmen Valley Chapel in my hometown of Colorado Springs. It was a sold-out show of 1,500 people and they were turning others away at the door. You could feel the energy in the room and knew these people were ready to laugh.

The show went great—we sold our products and headed home. I love shows like that because I can hang out with my friends whom I don't get to see too often and still be in bed with my wife that same night. It was just another show for me, but for someone else it had been a life-changing experience.

A week later, I got an e-mail from the promoter of the show. He said a lady had brought her 13-year-old autistic son to the show and that boy had never laughed before. He either didn't know how to laugh or maybe never had a reason to. That night, for the first time in the history of that boy's life, he laughed. Then he laughed some more. And some more. He laughed for most of the night. She said he'd been laughing all week at things that he had never reacted to before. The boy's life had been changed because God decided to use some guys who like telling jokes.

Humor can be a powerful tool when used the way God intended it. It can heal someone physically and emotionally.

One of my favorite pictures is of Jesus' face—and He's laughing. In heaven, we'll all be laughing.

15

GOD'S POWER

Power corrupts. Absolute power is kind of neat.
JOHN LEHMAN

God is sitting in heaven when a scientist says to Him, "Lord, we don't need You anymore. Science has finally figured out a way to create life out of nothing. In other words, we can now do what You did in the 'beginning.'"

"Oh, is that so? Tell me . . ." replies God.

"Well," says the scientist, "we can take dirt and form it into the likeness of You and breathe life into it, thus creating man."

"Well, that's interesting. Show Me."

So the scientist bends down to the earth and starts to mold the soil.

"Oh, no, no, no . . ." interrupts God. "Get your own dirt."

Words to Live By

*But you will receive power
when the Holy Spirit comes on you;
and you will be my witnesses in Jerusalem,
and in all Judea and Samaria,
and to the ends of the earth.*
ACTS 1:8, *NIV*

Just Some Ideas

One of the coolest things about being a Christian is that we have power through the Holy Spirit. God gives us this power to help us deal with temptation, various problems and when that one particular person just keeps bugging you.

A couple of months ago I did a show where Evander Holyfield was the main speaker of the night. During dinner I was able to talk to him about some of the things he had been through. I told him how much he had inspired me the first time he fought Mike Tyson, when he wore his robe with Philippians 4:13 ("I can do all things in him who strengthens me") printed on the back. I asked him what he had done to prepare that day. He said, "I spent the day praying for His power. I knew I had trained physically; now it was time to kneel down before my Jesus and ask for His power to complete the task."

Then onstage I made fun of Evander and he beat me up!

A lot of people who aren't Christians (and some who are) like to quote a particular verse in the Bible: "God helps those who help themselves." People like to quote this when they're trying to argue that God only helps us when we first try to do it ourselves. That particular verse is in the Book of Yo Mama, chapter 1. Ladies and gentlemen, contrary to popular belief, that quote is not in the Bible. Actually, Benjamin Franklin coined the phrase. The truth is, God helps us when we can't help ourselves and when we ask Him to help us.

Is there something in your life that you feel powerless to change? Ask God for help. He's completely willing to listen to anything you might have to say. Sit down and think about all the garbage in your life you'd like to clean up. Then ask God to do it. Ask Him for power to live each day in a way that is pleasing to Him—I guarantee He'll answer.

Prayer

God, I pray for Your power.
I pray for the grace to live a life that You can be proud of.
I give You my daily battles that You may deal with
them accordingly.
Lead me in the way of righteousness.
Amen.

16

CHARACTER

Too often when conscience tries to speak, the line seems to be busy.

Once upon a time there lived a woman named Robin who had a maddening passion for refried beans. She loved them, but unfortunately, they had always had a very embarrassing and somewhat lively reaction to her.

Then one day she met a guy and fell in love. When it became apparent that they would marry, she thought to herself, *He is so sweet and gentlemanly, he would never go for this bean business.* So she made the supreme sacrifice and gave up the beans.

Some months later, her car broke down on the way home from work. Since she lived in the country, she called her husband and told him that she would be late because she had to walk home. On her way, she passed a small diner and the odor of the refried beans was more than she could resist. Since she still had miles to walk, she figured that she would walk off any ill effects before she reached home.

So she stopped at the diner and before she knew it, she had consumed three large orders of refried beans. All the way home she putt-putted. And upon arriving home, she felt reasonably sure she could control it. Her husband seemed excited to see her and exclaimed delightedly, "Darling, I have a surprise for dinner tonight."

He then blindfolded her and led her to her chair at the table. She seated herself and just as her husband was about to remove her blindfold, the telephone rang. He made her promise not to touch the blindfold until he returned. He then went to answer the phone.

The refried beans she had consumed were still affecting her, and the pressure was becoming almost unbearable. So while her husband was out of the room, she seized the opportunity, shifted her weight to one leg and let it go. It was not only loud, but it also smelled like a fertilizer truck running over a skunk in front of pulpwood mill. She took her napkin and fanned the air around her vigorously. Then she shifted to the other cheek and ripped three more, which reminded her of cooked cabbage.

Keeping her ears tuned to the conversation in the other room, she went on like this for another 10 minutes. When the phone farewells signaled the end of her freedom, she fanned the air a few more times with her napkin, placed it on her lap and folded her hands upon it, smiling contentedly to herself. She was the picture of innocence when her husband returned— he apologized for taking so long. He then asked her if she had peeked, and she assured him that she had not.

At this point, he removed the blindfold, and she was surprised! There were 12 dinner guests seated around the table to wish her "Happy Birthday"!

Words to Live By

And not only this, but we also exult in our tribulations,
knowing that tribulation brings about perseverance;
and perseverance, proven character;
and proven character, hope;
and hope does not disappoint,
because the love of God has been poured out within our hearts
through the Holy Spirit who was given to us.

ROMANS 5:3-5

Just Some Ideas

Character can be defined as how you act when no one is watching. My character tends to suffer when I'm in traffic. I'll be praying about the day and get really upset that some guy cut me off. I'll pray, "Lord, thank You for today and all that You've given me. I pray for grace, love, purity . . . *get out of the way you stupid jerk! I will kill you!* . . . Amen." Or I'll be listening to some worship music and say, "Hallelujah to my savior . . . *get out of the left lane, you stupid old lady! You wanna fight right here? And turn off your blinker!* . . . Shout to the Lord, all the earth, let us sing!"

It's easy to be "Christian like" when you're in church or with friends. It's much simpler to be kind to other people when you're being watched by your peers. It's easier to give food to the poor when you're around people you're comfortable with. But when you're by yourself, you're as real as you possibly get.

What do you do when you're by yourself? Would you do those same things in public? Would God be proud of your actions?

If yes, then you're ahead of most people I know.

If not, then welcome to "Honesty 101"—and let's all resolve to start doing the things of God.

Prayer

God, I pray for uprightness of character when I'm alone.
I pray I would be the man or woman in private or in public
that You have called me to be.
Guide me in my walk with You and be with
me everywhere I go.
Amen.

17

ALCOHOL

Alcohol is like success:
Both are all right until they go to your head.

Every night, Frank would go down to the liquor store, get a bottle of liquor, bring it home and drink it while he watched TV. One night, as he finished his last drink, the doorbell rang. He stumbled to the door and found a six-foot-tall cockroach standing there. The bug grabbed him by the collar and threw him across the room, then left.

The next night, after Frank finished his fourth drink, the doorbell rang. He walked slowly to the door and found the same six-foot-tall cockroach standing there. The big bug punched him in the stomach, then left.

The next night, after he finished his first drink, the doorbell rang again. The same six-foot-tall cockroach was standing there. This time Frank was kneed in the groin and hit behind the ear as he doubled over in pain. Then the big bug left.

The fourth night Frank didn't drink at all. The doorbell rang. The cockroach was standing there. The bug beat the snot out of Frank and left him in a heap on the living room floor.

The following day, Frank went to see his doctor. He explained the events of the preceding four nights.

"What can I do?" he pleaded.

"Not much" the doctor replied. "There's just a nasty bug going around."

Words to Live By

Do not get drunk on wine, which leads to debauchery.
Instead, be filled with the Spirit.

EPHESIANS 5:18, *NIV*

Just Some Ideas

Alcohol is a big issue with our youth today. Apparently, to have a great time, you must drink to the point where you can't walk and then vomit continuously the day after. Boy, that sounds like a blast!

My father was in the military and I grew up in Germany, where the drinking age was 14. Sounds cool, right? I thought it was until I realized that our school had an Alcoholics Anonymous group with a number of members. I wonder how the meeting went. "Hi, my name is John, and I'm a freshman alcoholic." Was John there because he was a freshman or an alcoholic?

Personally, I've never been drunk in my life, not because I have incredible willpower, but because my father always said he would kill me if I did something stupid. I was unfortunate (or fortunate, however you look at it) in that I witnessed a number of my friends and family ruin their lives because of drinking. For each of them, it all started out so innocently. "It's only a couple, just to loosen up from a hard day" was what I would hear all the time. "I can't have any fun if I don't drink" was another one. My stand on drinking is that I don't think it's a sin, but I think it's wrong.

If you're a Christian, you have no business drinking. First Corinthians 6:12 says, "All things are lawful for me, but not all things are profitable. All things are lawful for me, but I will not be mastered by anything." If you want to drink, then don't be involved in a ministry at church. If some kid at church looks up to you and then sees you out somewhere with a beer in your hand, you've just taught a lesson to that child. What would you do if you saw Billy Graham drinking a beer? I would be crushed—as would almost every other person who has ever looked up to him.

I know, I know, pretty harsh stuff. But it's biblical and right. Whether you drink is up to you. You can have an amazing relationship with God and still drink casually, but in the end, it hurts more than it helps.

Prayer

Father, I pray that You would reveal to me whether it's
right to use alcohol.
I want to do Your will, so show me what I should do.
The world says it's okay to drink.
What do You say?
Amen.

18

THANKING GOD

*Most people repent of their sins
by thanking God they ain't so wicked as their neighbors.*
JOSH BILLINGS

Three people were on a plane. One said to the pilot, "I have a glass bottle. What do I do with it?" The pilot told him to throw it out the window.

The second one asked the same question, and the pilot also told him to throw it out the window.

The third one asked the pilot, "I have a bomb. What do I do with it?" The pilot told him to throw it out the window.

When they landed, they met a man who was crying. When asked why he was crying, he replied, "Because I got hit in the head with a glass bottle."

They met a woman who was crying for the same reason.

Then they the met a man who was laughing. They asked him why he was laughing, and he replied, "Because I walked by a building and passed gas. Then the building blew up."

Words to Live By

*He who observes the day, observes it for the Lord,
and he who eats, does so for the Lord, for he gives thanks to God;
and he who eats not, for the Lord he does not eat, and gives thanks to God.
For not one of us lives for himself, and not one dies for himself,*

for if we live, we live for the Lord, or if we die, we die for the Lord;
therefore, whether we live or die, we are the Lord's.

ROMANS 14:6-8

Just Some Ideas

Have you ever blamed God for the problems you have? We are notorious for absolving ourselves of blame for our problems. Usually we make our own messes but we can't admit it. And so we decide to place blame with the Almighty. How stupid. I mean, obviously God is out to get people!

I hear people all the time saying, "I'm so happy—things are working out." Then the next day, when things aren't going so well, they say, "Why is God punishing me?" Who said God was punishing you?

Here's an exercise for you: Take a look inward at yourself and you'll find that every problem you have has been caused by you—or an ex-girlfriend. The poor decisions you make in your life are the direct cause of any problems you have.

I'll let you in on a little secret: God does not have it in for you. God wants you to succeed. He urges you to ask Him for help and He will help you if it's in your best interest. And when He does allow you to succeed, thank Him with all your heart!

Prayer

Father, I thank You.
I thank You for all the successes and failures I've had.
I pray that You would guide me in every venture and lead
me where I should go.
I give You my life and submit to the will You have for me.
Amen.

PLEDGE OF ALLEGIANCE

With hurricanes, tornados, flooding, fires, severe thunderstorms and earthquakes tearing up the country from one end to another, are we sure this is a good time to take God out of the Pledge of Allegiance?
JAY LENO

A man carrying a Bible boards an airplane and sits next to an atheist. The man opens up his Bible and begins to read. The atheist glances at the Bible, looks straight ahead and then snickers loudly.

The Bible-reading man turns to him and says, "Is there something wrong?"

The atheist replies, "That book is nothing but made-up stories. Do you really believe everything in that book?"

"Well, yeah."

"Do you really believe that Moses parted the Red Sea?" the atheist asked.

"Of course I do."

"Well, what about that guy Jonah—do you really believe he was in the belly of a whale for three days and three nights?"

"Yes," the man said.

"Well, how did he do it?" the atheist countered.

"I don't know," the man replied. "But I'll tell you what: When I get to heaven, I'll ask him."

"What if he's not in heaven?" the atheist asked.

"Then you can ask him."

Words to Live By

What other nation is so great
as to have their gods near them
the way the LORD our God is near us
whenever we pray to him?

DEUTERONOMY 4:7

Just Some Ideas

For some reason, atheists are passionate about what they believe . . . or don't believe. I just don't get it. They want to prove to everyone that there is no God and we are all here by chance.

Have you ever met one of these people? You tell them you go to church and they explode into a rant about how religion has been the cause of every war and it's just an institution to control people.

I don't want to make fun of atheist people but . . . here we go!

Now they want to take the "under God" out of the Pledge of Allegiance. They say it's offensive to have those two words there because they don't agree with it. Here's my question: How can you be offended by something you don't believe in? Look, if you don't like the way we do things is this country, you are free to leave. (Seriously, you have that right—no matter how much we may want to, under the law we can't make you stay.)

Anyway, back to my point about the Pledge. Here's my opinion. I say, go ahead and remove the "under God" from the Pledge of Allegiance, but you're going to have to replace it with something, just to be fair to both sides. So here's my recommendation for the new Pledge of Allegiance:

I pledge allegiance to the flag of the United States of
America, and to the Republic for which it
stands, one nation . . .

Under a blue sky

Formed by chance

Through a random process of organization

Against incalculable odds

And in complete opposition to the laws of physics,
probability and entropy

Paying no attention to our forefathers who founded
this country on Christian principles

Without the aid or direction of any higher power

And for no reason whatsoever

Indivisible, with liberty and justice for all.

I rest my case.

Prayer

God, You are our Father and Creator.
I pray that we, as a nation, would turn to You for guidance
and that You would have mercy on us.
Forgive us for ignoring You and Your commandments.
Forgive us for removing You from the classroom
and for not praying to You in public because it's not
politically correct.
Help us draw close to You in unity to become a nation
wholly dedicated to You.

20

GREED

My mother taught me never to be greedy.
To teach me this lesson, she took my piggy bank.
RICH PRAYTOR

Recently a "Husband Shopping Center" opened in Phoenix where women could go to choose a husband from among many men. It was laid out in five floors, with the men increasing in positive attributes as you ascended.

The only rule was, once you opened the door to any floor, you *had* to choose a man from that floor. If you went up a floor, you couldn't go back down, except to leave the place, never to return.

A couple of girlfriends went to the shopping center to find some husbands . . .

First floor. The door had a sign saying, "These men have jobs and love kids." The women read the sign and said, "Well, that's better than not having a job, or not loving kids, but I wonder what's farther up." So up they went.

Second floor. The sign read, "These men have high-paying jobs, love kids and are extremely good looking." "Hmm," said the ladies. "But, I wonder what's farther up?"

Third floor. This sign read, "These men have high-paying jobs, are extremely good looking, love kids and help with the housework." "Wow!" said the women. "Very tempting, *but* there's more farther up!" And up they went.

Fourth floor. This door had a sign saying, "These men have high-paying jobs, love kids, are extremely good looking, help with the housework and have a strong romantic streak." "Oh, mercy me. But just think! What must be awaiting us farther on!" the ladies said. So up to the fifth floor they went.

Fifth floor. The sign on that door said, "This floor is empty and exists only to prove that women are impossible to please. Goodbye."

Words to Live By

Now the deeds of the flesh are evident, which are:
immorality, impurity, sensuality, idolatry, sorcery, enmities,
strife, jealousy, outbursts of anger, disputes, dissensions, factions,
envying, drunkenness, carousing, and things like these,
of which I forewarn you, as I have forewarned you,
that those who practice such things will not inherit the kingdom of God.

GALATIANS 5:19-21

Just Some Ideas

We humans are selfish by nature. It doesn't matter who you are, we are all selfish in one capacity or another. I'm an only child, so naturally I was spoiled growing up. Fortunately my father was very adamant about my not becoming a spoiled-rotten kid. So every time my parents gave me a present, they spanked me. I hated Christmas.

As Christians, we need to be unselfish in our daily lives. It sounds cliché to say this, but here are some reasons why being selfish is destructive. First, when people find out you have a selfish nature, they're inclined to treat you differently. Second, as unfair as it is, people will judge *all* Christians by the way *you* act. Remember, you are representing Christ—so if you are selfish, you are not being a pleasing witness. In fact, you are failing to fulfill your calling to spread the gospel.

How selfish are you? Do you routinely think, *How can I benefit from this?*

If so, one thing you can do that's extremely powerful is to ask God for humility. Ask God to change your way of thinking. Request that you would develop a heart for the people in your life and that you would serve them wholeheartedly. When you learn to be unselfish, you'll have more than you've ever wanted.

Prayer

Father, I pray that I would not be selfish.
Please change my heart so that I would live and love
in a way that honors You.
I pray that I would serve the people in my life
just as You would.
Make me an extension of Yourself,
and help me to treat people in such a way
that I lead them to You.
Amen.

21

MARRIAGE

My wife thinks I'm too nosy.
At least that's what she writes in her diary.
DRAKE SATHER

A young couple decided to get married. As the big day approached, they grew apprehensive. They both had a problem they had never before shared with anyone, not even each other. The groom-to-be, overcoming his fear, decided to ask his father for advice.

"Father," he said, "I am deeply concerned about the success of my marriage. I love my fiancée very much, but you see, I have very smelly feet, and I'm afraid that my future wife will be put off by them."

"No problem," said Dad. "All you have to do is wash your feet as often as possible, and always wear socks, even to bed."

Well, to him this seemed a workable solution. The bride-to-be, overcoming her fear, decided to take her problem to her mom. "Mom," she said, "when I wake up in the morning, my breath is horrific."

"Honey," her mother consoled, "everyone has bad breath in the morning."

"No, you don't understand. My morning breath is so bad that I'm afraid that my new husband will not want to sleep in the same bed with me."

Her mother said simply, "Try this. In the morning, get out of bed and head for the bathroom and brush your teeth. The key is not to say a word until you've brushed your teeth. Not a word," her mother affirmed.

Well, the bride-to-be thought it was certainly worth a try.

The couple was finally married in a beautiful ceremony. Not forgetting the advice they had received, he with his perpetual socks and she with her morning silence, they managed quite well. That is, until about six months later.

Before dawn, the husband awoke with a start to find that one of his socks had come off. Fearing the consequences, he frantically searched the bed.

This, of course, woke his bride and without thinking, she immediately asked, "What on Earth are you doing?"

"Oh, no!" he gasped in shock. "You've swallowed my sock!"

Words to Live By

Love is patient, love is kind and is not jealous;
love does not brag and is not arrogant,
does not act unbecomingly; it does not seek its own,
is not provoked, does not take into account a wrong suffered,
does not rejoice in unrighteousness, but rejoices with the truth;
bears all things, believes all things, hopes all things, endures all things.

1 CORINTHIANS 13:4-7

Just Some Ideas

Marriage is that wonderful institution that brings a man and a woman together for life, except in California. Today over half of all marriages (both Christian and not) end in divorce. Why? Because people don't understand what love is.

My parents have been married for 30 years. That's a lot of NBA playoff games. I asked my dad what the key to a long marriage was. He told me, "You have to understand that love is not an emotion; it's an action. There are some days that I don't 'feel' in love with your mom, but that doesn't mean I'm not. Once you can grasp that love is a decision, not a feeling, your marriage has a great chance of success."

I think a lot of marriages fail because people "fall out of love" with each other. They think that because they don't feel in love anymore, they're not. Instead of working through the issues of marriage, they move on through divorce or separation in search of that "feeling" again.

In my walk with Christ, I've struggled with this for a long time. At points, I haven't felt close to God, so I thought I wasn't. One day I realized that my emotions don't dictate my relationship with Him. It's okay to be sad or frustrated—and you don't have to wait until the negative feelings are gone to talk to God.

Do your emotions determine your walk with God? Have you ever said, "I don't feel close to God." Remember to, "with all prayer and petition, pray at all times in the Spirit" (Ephesians 6:18). Then watch your relationship with the Almighty reach new heights.

Prayer

Father, I pray that You would control my emotions
so that they won't dictate my life.
I pray that I would come to You at any point
in my day to worship You,
no matter how I feel. I worship You, Lord,
in my sadness and in my joy.
Amen.

CHILDLIKE

*My folks refuse to have more than four children
after reading that every fifth child born in the world is Chinese.*

A couple had two little boys, ages 8 and 10, who were excessively mischievous. They were always getting into trouble and their parents knew that if any mischief occurred in their town, their sons were probably involved.

The boys' mother heard that a pastor in town had been successful in disciplining children, so she asked if he would speak with her boys. The pastor agreed, but he asked to see them individually. So the mother sent her 8-year-old in the morning and then the older boy went to see the pastor in the afternoon.

The pastor, a huge man with a booming voice, sat the younger boy down and asked him sternly and with a mean scowl, "Where is God?"

The boy's mouth dropped open and his eyes opened wide, but he made no response. So the pastor repeated the question in an even sterner tone, "Where is God?!" Again the boy made no attempt to answer. So the pastor raised his voice even more and shook his finger in the boy's face and bellowed, *"Where is God?!"*

The boy screamed and bolted from the room, ran directly home and dove into his closet, slamming the door behind him. When his older brother found him in the closet, he asked, "What happened?"

The younger brother, gasping for breath, replied, "We are in *big* trouble this time, dude. God is missing—and they think *we* did it!"

Words to Live By

When Jesus saw this, He was indignant and said to them,
"Permit the children to come to Me; do not hinder them;
for the kingdom of God belongs to such as these."

MARK 10:14

Just Some Ideas

Remember the innocence we all had when we were kids? When
I was in fifth grade, I got a new bike for Christmas and started
riding it to school. One day after school I went to get my bike and
noticed that the grips on my handlebars were gone. I remember standing there trying to figure out what had happened to my
grips. At first I thought maybe I had put them in my backpack
and forgotten about them. Then I thought they had fallen off as
I rode to school that morning. It wasn't until my friend told
me that someone took them that I started to figure things out.
I thought, *Why would someone take my grips when they do not belong
to them?* Along with my bike grips, a small part of my innocence
was taken from me that day.

God wants us to be like children because they're so much
fun to be with. The simplest things make them happy. You
give them candy and they smile. You play them a song and they
dance without worrying who might be watching them. You
give them matches and they tell on you (not that that's ever
happened).

I want to encourage you to ask God to bring back that
childlike spirit you once had. Be like a kid in your walk with
Christ. Remember the little things He gives you every day and
smile like you mean it (except in the bathroom—there's no
smiling in the bathroom).

Keep in mind that God wants you to be happy. Just think of the happiest people on this earth: the children. And then remember what Jesus had to say about them (see Mark 10:14).

Prayer

Father, I pray that I would be childlike
in every sense of the word.
I pray for a humble heart in my walk with You,
that I would listen to Your direction
and be diligent in my efforts to spread the good news.
I give You my life for Your use.
Amen.

REMEMBERING GOD

When I think of my dad as a little boy,
I tend to think of him in black and white.

An elderly husband and wife are having problems remembering things, so they decide to go to their doctor to get checked out to make sure nothing is wrong with them. When they arrive at the doctor's, they explain to him that they are having problems with their memory.

After examining the couple, the doctor tells them that they are physically fine but that they might want to start writing things down and make notes to help them recall things. The couple thanks the doctor and then leaves.

Later that night while watching TV, the old man gets up from his chair and his wife asks, "Where are you going?"

He replies, "To the kitchen."

She asks, "Will you get me a bowl of ice cream?"

He replies, "Sure."

She then asks him, "Don't you think you should write it down so that you can remember it?"

He says, "No, I can remember that."

She then says, "Well, I also would like some strawberries on top. You had better write that down because I know you'll forget that."

He says, "I can remember that, you want a bowl of ice cream with strawberries."

She replies, "Well, I also would like whipped cream on top. I know you will forget that, so you better write it down."

With irritation in his voice, he says, "I don't need to write that down—I can remember that." He then fumes into the kitchen.

After about 20 minutes, he returns from the kitchen and hands her a plate of bacon and eggs. She stares at the plate for a moment and says, "You forgot my toast."

Words to Live By

Be careful that you do not forget the LORD your God.
DEUTERONOMY 8:11, *NIV*

Just Some Ideas

When I was a kid, I loved drinking milk before going to bed. One night I drank only half of what had been given to me, and I left the remaining glass of milk on my dresser next to my bed. I forgot about it until three days later. When I noticed it, I thought, *Hey, I'll drink the rest of it right now.* As I tilted the glass toward my face, this blob of rotten milk crashed into my face with all the stench of a vulture's breath. After that, I never forgot to finish my glass of milk at bedtime!

I know sometimes we forget God. I know I get caught up in doing so much "Christian stuff" that I forget the reason I'm doing it. I forget all the miracles I've seen in my life. I lose track of all the amazing blessings I've had over the years and take for granted what I have now.

Do you forget about God sometimes? If so, then admit it and move one. Don't dwell on it—just get on your knees and start praying to your Savior. Make it a point to spend time with Him every day and never forget how good He's been to you.

Prayer

*Father, I pray that I will remember You in
everything that I do.
I pray You will remind me of all the
great things in my life.
Please help me to remember Your sacrifice
for me on the cross
and help me to look to You for guidance.
Amen.*

PRIORITIES

Honk if you like peace and quiet.

One day in the Garden of Eden, Eve calls out to God, "Lord, I have a problem!"

"What's the problem, Eve?"

"Lord, I know You've created me and have provided this beautiful garden and all of these wonderful animals, and that hilarious comedic snake, but I'm just not happy."

"Why is that, Eve?" comes the reply from above.

"Lord, I am lonely. And I'm sick to death of apples."

"Well, Eve, in that case, I have a solution. I shall create a man for you."

"What's a 'man,' Lord?"

"This man will be a flawed creature, with many bad traits. He'll lie, cheat and be vainglorious; all in all, he'll give you a hard time. But, he'll be bigger, faster and will like to hunt and kill things—so he'll provide for you. He'll be witless and will revel in childish things like fighting and kicking a ball about. He won't be too smart, so he'll need your advice to think properly."

"Sounds great," says Eve, with an ironically raised eyebrow. "What's the catch, Lord?"

"Yeah, well, you can have him on one condition."

"What's that, Lord?"

"As I said, he'll be proud, arrogant and self-admiring. So you'll have to let him believe that I made him first. So, just remember . . . . it's our secret—woman to woman!"

Words to Live By

And the angel said to her,
"Do not be afraid, Mary, for you have found favor with God.
And behold, you will conceive in your womb and bear a son,
and you shall name Him Jesus.
He will be great, and will be called the Son of the Most High;
and the Lord God will give Him the throne of his father David;
and he will reign over the house of Jacob forever,
and His kingdom will have no end."

LUKE 1:30-33

Just Some Ideas

I grew up in a very Catholic home. My mom had crucifixes on the wall, paintings of all the saints and a Pope John Paul II air freshener. I was also brought up to hold Mary (the mother of Jesus) in very high regard, high enough to even have a statue of her and say some prayers in hope she would intercede for me.

Now, a lot of non-Catholics would openly disagree with the way my mom revered Mary. But my stance is that *anything* that gets in the way of God needs to be removed. I've seen a lot of non-Catholics worship things and people (that aren't Mary) more than God. I've seen people hold their pastor in such high regard that I question who they like more, him or God. I've seen worship bands singing songs to God but worshiping themselves. I've seen people get so involved in "doing church" that when God is mentioned, eyes start to roll. It's a little too ironic—don't you think (thanks, Alanis!).

What in your life is number one? Is God really the most important person in your life? Are there things that are more important?

I know in my life that it's a constant struggle to keep my priorities straight. Some days are great, some days I fail. But the reason God is so great is that when we fail, He meets us right where we are and showers us with His grace.

Prayer

I pray that I would keep You number one in my life.
I pray for the wisdom to know when I need to
make changes in my life
that would honor You. Help me get rid of the
things that keep me from You.
I pray for Your grace, that You would give it
to me every day
so that I can worship You forever.
Amen.

REPUTATION

Reputation is character minus what you've been caught doing.
MICHAEL IAPOCE

A lady bought a new Lexus. It cost a bundle. Two days later, she brought it back complaining that the radio wasn't working.

"Madam," said the sales manager, "the audio system in this car is completely automated. All you need to do is tell it what you want to listen to, and you will hear exactly that!"

She drove out, somewhat amazed and a little confused. She looked at the radio and said, "Nelson."

The radio responded, "Ricky or Willie?" Soon she was speeding down the highway to the sounds of "On the Road Again." The lady was astounded. If she wanted Beethoven, that's what she got. If she wanted Nat King Cole, she got it.

At the next intersection, when her light turned green, she pulled out. Off to her right, out of the corner of her eye, she saw a small SUV speeding toward her. She swerved and narrowly missed a collision.

"Moron," she muttered.

And from the radio came, "Ladies and gentlemen, Homer Simpson . . ."

Words to Live By

And he must have a good reputation with those outside the church,
so that he will not fall into reproach and the snare of the devil.

1 TIMOTHY 3:7

Just Some Ideas

Have you ever heard something about a person and made a judgment about that person's character before you even met him or her? I know I have. Or have you ever done something wrong and then later been labeled "the person who did that bad thing"? It's human nature to look at the flaws and failings of other people to help us feel better about ourselves. It's sad but true.

But here's something you might want to remember: Your reputation is one of the single most important things you have in your life. A great reputation can bring you friends, wealth and happiness throughout your life. A bad reputation can take all those things away.

Jesus called us to be "above reproach," which means "without blame" or "blameless." We're called to be without blame so that we can be better witnesses for Christ. The older you get, the more you'll realize that reputation is extremely important in your walk with Jesus.

Take the time to reflect on your life and the things in it that might be questionable in the eyes of others. Are there things you need to remove from your life? Is there something you can do better? I encourage you to take action because your reputation will directly affect how those around you think about Jesus.

Prayer

Father, teach me how to be a reputable person.
Show me how to honor You with my work and personal life.
I pray that I would be a solid witness for Your testimony
and never bring shame to Your name.
Amen.

26

HEART OF A CHILD

*Let's face it, there's a lot of spoiled kids out there . . .
because you can't spank grandma.*
JANET ANDERSON

I believe you should live each day as if it is your last, which is
why I don't have any clean laundry because, come on, do I really
want to spend the last day of my life doing the wash?
—Age 15

Give me the strength to change the things I can, the grace to
accept the things I cannot and a great big bag of money.
—Age 13

Democracy is a beautiful thing, except for that part about letting
just any old yokel vote.
—Age 10

For centuries, people thought the moon was made of green cheese.
Then the astronauts found that the moon is really a big hard
rock. That's what happens to cheese when you leave it out.
—Age 6

Think of the biggest number you can. Now add five. Then imagine if you had that many Twinkies. Wow, that's five more than
the biggest number you could come up with!
—Age 6

As you make your way through this hectic world of ours, set aside a few minutes each day. At the end of the year, you'll have a couple of days saved up.
—Age 7

Often, when I am reading a good book, I stop and thank my teacher. That is, I used to, until she got an unlisted number.
—Age 15

It would be terrible if the Red Cross Bloodmobile got into an accident. No, wait. That would be good because if anyone needed it, the blood would be right there.
—Age 5

If we could just get everyone to close their eyes and visualize world peace for an hour, imagine how serene and quiet it would be until the looting started.
—Age 15

Words to Live By

And he said: "I tell you the truth, unless you change
and become like little children,
you will never enter the kingdom of heaven."
MATTHEW 18:3, *NIV*

Just Some Ideas

Don't you love the innocence and honesty of children? A two-year-old can run around in the front yard naked and the neighbors say, "Oh, how adorable." If you're 29 years old and you do that, the neighbors call the cops.

Children call things as they see them. If you do something wrong, they call you on it. They don't get caught up in trying to rationalize the mistake—they just say, "Yeah, Daddy did it— I saw him."

Sometimes when I pray to God, I try to *explain* my sins to Him, as if I could somehow convince my Creator that my intentions were pure (when of course they weren't). Have you ever done that? Why do we try to fool God?

I encourage you this next week to look at the details of your life. If you were to have a seven-year-old spend an entire day with you, going everywhere with you, would that kid call you on something—and say something to embarrass you? If so, you might want to reconsider some of the things you might be doing. Be honest with yourself, and ask God to give you the heart of a child again. It's one of the most mature things you can do.

Prayer

Father, make me like a child again
in my life and in my heart.
Help me to see things like a child
so that I will make honest and pure decisions.
I come to You as a child and worship You,
my Father and Protector.
Amen.

27

SCIENCE AND THE BIBLE

I wanted to become an atheist but I gave it up.
They have no holidays.
ERICA JONG

A crocodile cannot stick out its tongue.

A snail can sleep for three years.

All polar bears are left-handed.

American Airlines saved $40,000 in 1987 by eliminating one olive from each salad served in first-class.

Americans on average eat 18 acres of pizza every day.

An ostrich's eye is bigger than its brain.

Babies are born without kneecaps. They don't appear until the child reaches two to six years of age.

Butterflies taste with their feet.

Cats have over 100 vocal sounds; dogs have only about 10.

China has more English speakers than the United States.

Donald Duck comics were banned in Finland because he doesn't wear any pants.

Elephants are the only animals that can't jump.

February 1865 is the only month in recorded history not to have a full moon.

If you yelled for 8 years, 7 months and 6 days, you will have produced enough sound energy to heat one cup of coffee.

Leonardo da Vinci invented scissors.

No word in the English language rhymes with "month."

Nutmeg is extremely poisonous if injected intravenously.

Our eyes are always the same size from birth, but our nose and ears never stop growing.

Right-handed people live, on average, nine years longer than left-handed people.

Shakespeare invented the words "assassination" and "bump."

Starfish haven't got brains.

The ant always falls over on its right side when intoxicated.

The catfish has over 27,000 taste buds.

The cruise ship the Queen Elizabeth II moves only six inches for each gallon of diesel that it burns.

The names of all the continents end with the same letter they start with.

The name "Wendy" was made up for the book *Peter Pan*.

The strongest muscle in the body is the tongue.

There are two credit cards for every person in the United States.

"Typewriter" is the longest word that can be made using the letters on only one row of the keyboard.

Women blink nearly twice as much as men.

And finally . . .

You are more likely to be killed by a champagne cork than by a poisonous spider.

Words to Live By

Is it by your understanding that the hawk soars,
stretching his wings toward the south?
Is it at your command that the eagle mounts up
and makes his nest on high?
On the cliff he dwells and lodges, upon the rocky crag,
an inaccessible place.
From there he spies out food; his eyes see it from afar.

JOB 39:26-29

Just Some Ideas

I love these verses because they prove the existence of God. Back in the 1950s, scientists established the fact that eagles hunt for food using their sharp eyesight (before that time it was believed that they hunted by smell). If you look at this verse in Job, which was written about 3,000 years before Christ, it explains that an eagle "spies out the food; his eyes see it from afar." This makes me realize that since the beginning of time, God has really known what He's been talking about.

Here's another tidbit for the "fun fact" category in your brain. Science says that something cannot come from nothing. When you leave a piece of meat out in the sun and maggots appear a couple of days later, the meat didn't produce them—nope, it was the flies that landed on the meat. The flies laid eggs in the meat, resulting in a maggot party. This is just one of many pieces of evidence that support Louis Pasteur's "law of biogenesis": Life only comes from life. So why do scientists today still back the Big Bang theory? Scientists say that in the vast nothingness of the universe, a huge explosion happened (for no apparent reason), and life was created. So something came from nothing? And they say the Bible contradicts itself!

Do you sometimes have trouble believing that the Bible is true? If you do, then don't worry—you're not alone. But in reality, the Bible is full of scientific truth. I advise you to seek out books that address the relationship between science and the Bible, such as Lee Strobel's *The Case for a Creator*. Or get on the Internet and look up "Bible" and "scientific fact"—you'll find dozens of articles proving the accuracy of the Bible. Seek out the truth and God will reveal some amazing things to you.

Prayer

Father, open my eyes to the
wonderful things in Your Word.
Reveal to me the truths You want me to know
about You and Your creation.
Thank You for giving me life; in return,
I give myself to Your will.
Amen.

WHITE LIES

A lie gets halfway around the world
before the truth has a chance to get its pants on.
SIR WINSTON CHURCHILL

A 1990 article by Richard Waller, published in *Spy* magazine, made some interesting observations about Santa Claus.

First, according to the Population Reference Bureau, there are about 2 billion children (small people under the age of 18) in the world. Because Santa doesn't seem to handle the kids in the non-Western world, that leaves him with about 378 million children to visit on Christmas Eve. At a rate of, say, 3.5 children per household, that's 91.8 million homes.

Assuming that Santa travels from east to west, he has about 31 hours of Christmas time to visit all of these children (this is due to the different time zones and the rotation of the earth). This works out to roughly 822.6 visits per second. That means that for each household, Santa has 1/1000th of a second to park the sleigh, jump down the chimney, fill the stockings, put presents under the tree, eat any snacks, kiss Mommy (when available), get back up the chimney, hop in the sleigh and move on.

Now, if we assume that these 91.8 million stops are evenly distributed around the earth, we're now talking about 0.78 miles per household—a total trip of 75.5 million miles, not counting stops to let Santa and the reindeer do what most of us must do at least once every 31 hours. This means Santa's sleigh must move at a rate of 650 miles per second. (A conventional reindeer, by the way, can run 15 miles per hour, or 18 miles per hour with Nikes.)

If we next assume that each child gets nothing more than a medium-sized Lego set (weighing two pounds), Santa's sleigh would be carrying approximately 321,300 tons of goodies (not counting an overweight Santa). Even granting that flying reindeer can pull 10 times the amount of ordinary reindeer (which can pull no more than 300 pounds), Santa would need 214,200 reindeer. This increases the payload (not counting the sleigh or any snow that might be lingering on it) to 353,430 tons, or 4 times the weight of the Queen Elizabeth II.

Of course, that much weight traveling that fast would create an enormous amount of air resistance, which would then heat the reindeer to incandescence in the same fashion as spacecraft or meteors entering the earth's atmosphere. The lead pair of reindeer would absorb 14.3 quintillion joules of energy, per second, each. In short, they would burst into flame almost instantaneously, vaporizing the entire team within 4.26 thousandths of a second.

Meanwhile, jolly ol' St. Nick would be subjected to centrifugal forces in the amount of 17,500.06 gravities. A 250-pound Santa (a wee bit of an underestimate) would be pinned to the back of his sleigh by the 4,315,015 pounds of force.

Mr. Waller's conclusion to the above was that "if Santa ever did deliver presents on Christmas Eve, he's dead now."[1]

Words to Live By

But for the cowardly and unbelieving . . . and all liars,
their part will be in the lake that burns with fire and brimstone,
which is the second death.

REVELATION 21:8

Just Some Ideas

I remember the day I found out that there was no Santa Claus. I was coming home from college and . . . actually, I was in my fifth-grade Sunday School class when the teacher said, "So we all know that there's no Santa Claus, right?" I was crushed. I wondered, *Why would my parents lie to me about that? In fact, why did all parents lie to their kids about that? Why is everyone lying?* Then they told us kids never to lie because it's wrong. Hello!? Can you see the discrepancy here?

The Bible comes down pretty hard on the lying issue because if someone lies, that person is being deceitful about something. And being deceitful is bad. There's nothing worse than when someone you trust lies to your face. It almost physically hurts because all trust has been immediately broken. It's difficult to forgive someone who lies, because in the back of your mind, there's doubt as to whether you can trust this person in the future.

How often do you lie? Maybe you tell a little white lie or you lie blatantly. We all tend to exaggerate the truth from time to time to make our stories a little bit funnier so that our friends will like us more. But what we're talking about here is telling deliberate untruth. The Bible tells us all liars go to "H-E-double hockey sticks," so obviously doing the deed of lying is bad. (Of course, you all know the Bible also tells us that all liars on Earth dwell in one place: Congress).

Is there a certain situation in which you tend to lie most often? Then take the time to ask God about the issue and work through it. Ask Him for conviction when you say something that's not quite true. In the end, you'll be thankful that you've been honest with yourself, your Creator and the IRS.

Prayer

I pray for an honest heart, mind and soul.
I pray that I would be truthful in everything that I say or do.
I pray my words would be honest and forthright
and pleasing to You.
Convict me when I need to be corrected,
and give me the grace to be honest with myself,
my family and You.
Amen.

Note
1. Richard Waller,
   "Is There a Santa Claus?"
   Spy magazine,
   January 1990.

HOW I MET THE LOVE OF MY LIFE

I've had two dreams in my life that God, in His wisdom and grace, has made come true. The first dream was to land a job as a comedian. The day I left my cubicle (when they escorted me from the building) was a great day. I know God has called me to make people laugh and think through comedy, TV and films. I didn't know that being a comedian would directly impact my second dream.

My second dream was to meet, fall in love with and marry a hot Christian girl. As shallow as that sounds, that was my desire. Maybe it was because I was a tall, skinny dork in high school and never had a girlfriend. Or because my acne and braces repelled both women and mosquitoes.

I would lay on my roof every night in the summer and dream of being a comedian and making people laugh. I'd also dream of coming home to a gorgeous wife who thought I was the funniest person ever to walk in our zip code. We'd have two beautiful kids and enough money to travel anywhere and anytime we wanted. I'd have to put on a hat and sunglasses in the airport so that I wouldn't get mobbed by fans—and my kids would tell their friends that their father was the reason the Cold War ended.

Okay, I can walk through the airport without getting mob-bed, except in the security line when I forget to remove my knife from my carry-on. And the Cold War *is* over—but I had nothing to do with it. (I think *Rocky IV* gets credit for that one.) And I don't have enough money to travel whenever I want to. My wife and I go on vacation after we see my travel schedule for work and decide where we'll stay for a couple of extra days. Usually it's Orlando or San Francisco or, if I'm having a bad year, Biloxi!

But getting back to how my first dream impacted my sec-ond dream . . . You see, I work mostly weekends. Now, most people work during the week and socialize on the weekends. Because of my schedule, I missed a lot of social events and didn't make it to church on a consistent basis. So here I was doing what I loved to do but not having any opportunity to meet peo-ple that I could date.

So one night out on the road, I was watching a news story about online dating. I'd heard of online dating before—mainly all the horror stories! I'd been told one story about a man who finally arranged to meet in person a woman he'd been e-mailing. They met at a coffee shop, and she ended up kidnapping him and taking him to Venezuela for six months. I knew I didn't want to go to Venezuela, especially if it meant being brought there by force by my new girlfriend. That's not a great way to start a relationship.

But this news story mentioned a lot of actors and famous people who were choosing to meet people online because it was easy—and because their schedules didn't allow them time for "traditional dating." Well, that was enough for me! So the next day I signed up to look for my love online.

Little did I know that there are a lot of people who exagger-ate their dating profiles. One lady told me she was a CPA. Later I found out she meant a Certified Parking Attendant. Another lady was looking to get married in two months because her work visa was going to expire. When I told her I wasn't interested, she accused me of being afraid of commitment. I said, "No, I'm afraid of commitment to you."

If there's one piece of advice I can give you about online dating, it's this: Post a recent picture of yourself. Recent doesn't mean within the last 10 years! And don't get your friend who's talented with Photoshop to "slim down" your gut. The more honest you are about yourself at first, the better luck you'll have finding someone.

One day I got this e-mail from a girl who lived five miles away. She said, "Hi, I liked your profile and saw that you live in the area. Maybe we can meet for coffee." I checked out her picture and she was very pretty. I'm thinking, *Okay, there's got to be something wrong with her.* But I went ahead and e-mailed her back.

We ended up chatting on the phone the next day for an hour. She was fun, intelligent and had a great sense of humor. It thought to myself, *She's really fun to talk to. She has a great personality. She must be making up for something. Maybe she has vampire teeth or only one eye.* But I took a chance.

Here's another piece of advice if you're going to date online: Meet for coffee on your first date. That way if things aren't going well, you can take off anytime. And it's a cheap date. (Of course, if you meet at Starbucks, it's about the same price as a dinner for two at a nice steak house.)

We met after church at the local coffee house just a few blocks away from my house. I got there early, not trying to get my hopes up about this girl. And I was being careful—I had given my roommate the American Embassy's number in Venezuela just in case I didn't come home that day.

When she walked in, I didn't realize it was her because I thought, *There's no way a girl like that would have trouble dating.* She was 6′ 1″, wearing trendy jeans, sandals and a sleeveless black shirt. (I had had a crush on Wonder Woman when I was a kid and all those feelings came rushing back in that instant.) She said, "You must be Rich." I thought, *No, I must be dreaming*. I was finally able to utter some words I can't remember right off hand, but they must have been understandable because we both got our coffee and sat down.

Seven hours later, I dropped her off at her car back at the coffee shop. We had gone to the beach, eaten lunch, walked in the sand, hiked a trail in a park, had dinner and walked on the beach again. At her car, we made plans to go to the beach again the next day. I knew my second dream was coming true.

That night I went home and logged off permanently from the dating site. I knew there was no one else I wanted to be with except her. I sat back thinking that if I hadn't been open to new ideas, I would have never met my bride-to-be.

God taught me a great lesson that Sunday night: When we follow God's plan for our lives, He never lets us down. I knew from Scripture that I needed a woman who put God first, so that's what I'd been seeking. God not only gave me the "hot Christian girl" I asked for, but He also put a woman in my life who makes me a better person. God knew exactly what I needed and allowed me to have it in His timing, not mine.

Don't worry about the things you don't have right now. In time, they will come. When you're obedient to God, He keeps His promise to give you the desires of your heart.

THE CROSS

*It means the verdict which God will pronounce over us
on the Day of Judgment
has been brought into the present.
We therefore do not need to fear the Judgment Day.*
ANTHONY HOEKEMA

A 10-year-old boy was failing math. His parents had tried every-thing from tutors to hypnosis, but with no success. Finally, at the urging of a family friend, they decided to enroll their son in a private school highly regarded for its high moral standards and its focus on supporting loving families.

After the first day, the boy's parents were surprised when he walked in after school with a stern, focused and very deter-mined expression on his face. He went straight past them, right to his room and quietly closed the door. For nearly two hours he toiled away in his room with math books strewn about his desk and the surrounding floor.

He emerged long enough to eat, and after quickly cleaning his plate, he went straight back to his room, closed the door and worked feverishly at his studies until bedtime. This pattern of behavior continued until it was time for the first quarter's report card. The boy walked in with it unopened, laid it on the dinner table and went straight to his room. Cautiously, his mother opened it and, to her amazement, she saw a large red "A" under the "Math" subject heading.

Overjoyed, she and her husband rushed into their son's room, thrilled at his remarkable progress.

"Was it the nuns that did it?" the father asked.

The boy shook his head and said, "No."

Next the father asked, "Was it the one-to-one tutoring? The peer-mentoring?"

Again the boy said, "No."

Surprised, the father continued probing, "The textbooks? The teachers? The curriculum?"

Yet again the son said, "No. But on that first day, when I walked in the front door and saw that guy nailed to the plus sign, I *knew* they meant business!"

Words to Live By

For it was the Father's good pleasure
for all the fullness to dwell in Him,
and through Him to reconcile all things to Himself,
having made peace through the blood of His cross;
through Him, I say, whether things on earth or things in heaven.
And although you were formerly alienated and
hostile in mind, engaged in evil deeds,
yet He has now reconciled you in His fleshly body through death,
in order to present you before Him holy and
blameless and beyond reproach.

COLOSSIANS 1:19-22

Just Some Ideas

The Cross. Jesus died on it. We wear the cross around our neck. My mother had a lot of crosses at our house growing up. She had one in every room to remind our family that Jesus had died for all of us. It was probably overkill, but I still felt safe because I knew vampires would never come to my home!

As I read more about the crucifixion and the meaning that it holds, I realize that even though it's a tragic story, it's one of the greatest events in human history. Here was an innocent Man who was beaten and wrongly accused (simply for trying to help people), and He never spoke a harsh word to anyone. From the beginning, He knew He was going to die this way. And in the end, He faced the humiliation of the cross like a true Savior, because He knew the eternal fate of all of humankind was resting on His shoulders.

How do you view the cross and the death of Jesus? Do you think of it as tragic or something great? What's your perception of Jesus Christ right now? When you think of Jesus, what comes to mind? Once you come to know who Jesus really was—and the significance of what He did for us—then you can begin to pursue a deep and intimate relationship with Him.

Prayer

Jesus, thank You for dying on the cross for me.
I know I don't truly understand the depth
and pain You went through
when it happened, but know I appreciate Your sacrifice.
Thank You for the gift of salvation and all that it brings.
I pray for the strength to face the trials ahead
and the ability to keep You at the center of my life.
Amen.

SUBMITTING TO LEADERSHIP

Being in politics is like being a football coach.
You have to be smart enough to understand the game,
and dumb enough to think it's important.
EUGENE McCARTHY

If Noah had built the Ark in A.D. 2000 . . .

And the Lord spoke to Noah and said, "In six months I'm going to make it rain until the whole earth is covered with water and all the evil people are destroyed. But I want to save a few good people, and two of every kind of living thing on the planet. You are commanded to build an Ark."

And in a flash of lightning, He delivered the specifications for the Ark.

"Okay," said Noah, nervously fumbling with the blueprints.

"Six months, and it starts to rain," the Lord reminded him. "Please have the Ark completed, or all of you will be swimming for a very long time."

Six months passed, the skies clouded up, and rain began to fall. The Lord saw that Noah was sitting in his front yard weeping. And there was no Ark.

"Noah," said the Lord. "Where is the Ark?"

"Lord, please forgive me!" begged Noah. "I did my best, but there were big problems. First, I had to get a building permit for the Ark construction process, and your plans didn't meet code. I had to hire an engineer to redraw the plans. Then I got in a big fight over whether the Ark needed a fire sprinkler system. Then my neighbor objected, claiming I was violating zoning by building the Ark in my front yard. I had to get a variance from the City Commission.

"Then I had problems getting enough wood for the Ark, because there was a ban on cutting trees in an effort to save the spotted owl. I had to convince the U.S. Fish and Wildlife Commission that I needed the wood to save the owls, but they wouldn't let me catch the owls, so, no owls.

"Then the carpenters formed a union and went on strike. I had to negotiate a settlement with the National Labor Relations Board before anyone would pick up a saw or hammer. Now we have 16 carpenters going on the boat, but no owls.

"Then I started gathering up the animals, and I got sued by an animal rights group. They objected to my taking only two of each kind.

"Just when I got the suit dismissed, the EPA notified me that I couldn't complete the Ark without filing an environmental impact statement on your proposed flood plan. They didn't take kindly to the idea that they had no jurisdiction over the conduct of a Supreme Being.

"Then the Army Corps of Engineers wanted a map of the proposed flood plan. I sent them a globe.

"Right now I'm trying to resolve a complaint from the Equal Employment Opportunity Commission over how many Croatians I'm supposed to hire.

"The IRS has seized all my assets, claiming I'm trying to avoid paying taxes by leaving the country.

"And I just got notice from the state about owing some kind of use tax. I really don't think I can finish the Ark for at least another five years," Noah wailed.

The sky began to clear.

The sun began to shine, and a rainbow arched across the sky. Noah looked up and smiled.

"You mean You're not going to destroy the earth?" he asked hopefully.

"No," said the Lord sadly. "The government already has."

Words to Live By

Every person is to be in subjection to the governing authorities,
for there is no authority except from God,
and those which exist are established by God.
Therefore whoever resists authority has opposed the ordinance of God;
and they who have opposed will receive condemnation upon themselves.

ROMANS 13:1-2

Just Some Ideas

How difficult is it to be an American Christian is today's world, with today's government? You've got a bunch of people in Washington, D.C., with their own political agendas trying to get things done their way. We have presidents that do "unofficial" business behind closed doors, according to the detailed reports in every major newspaper in America. Every time there is an election, mud-slinging politicians come out and try to convince you how great they are by promising the impossible.

With all this nonsense, what should we do as Christians? I mean, we have been commanded to support our leaders. The Bible specifically tells us that God is the One who puts people in their governing positions. He's the One who puts the presidents and princes into place. We must support our leaders, whether or not we agree with them.

As I write this book, the war in Iraq has "officially" been finished for almost two months. I don't know what to think about our involvement there. One side of me agrees with it; the other side doesn't. Since my father was over there fighting, I especially wanted it to end immediately. But through it all, I've stood by President Bush, not because I agree with him, but because he's our leader right now and I have been called to stand by him.

What view do you have of authority? Do you live by the biblical mandate that you must support your civic leaders? Or do you dismiss it as something that doesn't apply to you?

I would encourage you to keep abreast of current affairs—to be "in the know" about who is in authority over our country and world. Also I would encourage you to pray for your leaders on a regular basis. Pray for your president, member of Congress, and any other leader you can think of. They need your prayers just as much as you do. Your vote counts, but your prayers are something that will count even more in the end.

Prayer

*I pray for the humility to be a servant to my leaders,
whether to the leader of my country or the leader
of my department at work.
And let me be a loyal worker. Thank You for the
leaders I have now—
I pray I will serve them as You have called us to do.
And thank You, Jesus, for the being the
greatest servant of all.
Amen.*

31

SMALL THINGS COUNT

*We can do no great things;
only small things with great love.*
MOTHER TERESA

Father Alan Schlines woke up Sunday morning to find an exceptionally beautiful and sunny spring day had dawned. He knew he just had to play golf. So . . . he told the associate pastor that he was feeling sick and could not say Mass that day.

As soon as the associate pastor left the room, Father Schlines headed out of town to a golf course about 40 miles away. This way he knew he wouldn't accidentally meet anyone he knew from his parish. Setting up on the first tee, he was alone. After all, it was Sunday morning and everyone else was in church—so there was no chance of being caught!

About this time, St. Peter leaned over to the Lord while looking down from the heavens and exclaimed, "You're not going to let him get away with this, are you?"

The Lord sighed and said, "No, I guess not."

Just then Father Schlines hit the ball and it shot straight toward the pin, dropping just short of it, rolled up and fell into the hole. *It was a 420-yard hole-in-one!*

St. Peter was astonished. He looked at the Lord and asked, "Why did you let him do that?"

The Lord smiled and replied, "Who's he gonna tell?"

Words to Live By

He who is faithful in a very little thing is faithful also in much;
and he who is unrighteous in a very little thing is
unrighteous also in much.
Therefore if you have not been faithful in the use of
unrighteous wealth,
who will entrust the true riches to you?

LUKE 16:10-11

Just Some Ideas

In anything you want to do in your life, you have to start at the bottom. You have to learn the basics, work your way up and show your superiors that you know what you're doing. When I first started doing stand-up comedy, I promoted a show at our local coffee house. I took flyers to every church in the city and told all my friends to come.

The big night came and a whopping seven people showed up to see the show. I was so upset that I almost snuck away and drove home. But I didn't. My youth pastor prayed with us in the parking lot before the show and encouraged me to "be faithful in the little things."

That night was one of the best shows I had had up to that point in my life. Little did I know, there was a promoter in the audience who had just happened to stop by to see the show. She called me later and asked if I would open up for Five Iron Frenzy, a little band that was coming to town.

I ended up doing terribly at that concert, but that's not the point. The point is, because I had been faithful to my responsibilities, my territory was enlarged, so to speak. God met my obedience with an opportunity to further my career.

To be a "good" Christian, we must be faithful in the small stuff. We have to accomplish the things no one wants to do in order to obtain the things we're striving for.

I once had a friend who wanted to be a youth leader, so he asked the pastor if he could help out at the church. The pastor said, "Sure, come on by this week." So my friend showed up ready to preach, and the pastor said, "Thanks for coming. Go ahead and set up the chairs for the kids." You've got to be faithful in the small stuff.

Do you expect to do great things without paying your dues first? Is there something you could be doing that you don't think is important? If so, then take the initiative and be great in the small things. Do the little stuff to the best of your ability and develop a solid work ethic now. As you go through life, you'll come to realize how important small things are in your quest for the big prize.

Prayer

I pray that I will be faithful in the small things.
I pray I wouldn't brush them aside because
I feel they're not important.
Give me the discipline to complete each task,
whether big or small,
to the best of my ability.
I give You all that I do for Your glory.
Amen.

32

HONOR YOUR PARENTS

*When I was a boy of 14, my father was so ignorant
I could hardly stand to have the old man around.
But when I got to be 21,
I was astonished at how much the old man
had learned in 7 years.*
JOSH BILLINGS

Recently, a certain private school was faced with a unique problem.

A number of 12-year-old girls were beginning to use lipstick and would put it on in the bathroom. That was fine, but after they put on their lipstick, they would press their lips to the mirror, leaving dozens of little lip prints. Every night the maintenance man would remove them and the next day the girls would put them back.

Finally the principal decided that something had to be done. She called all the girls into the bathroom and met them there with the maintenance man. She explained that all these lip prints were causing a major problem for the custodian who had to clean the mirrors every night.

To demonstrate how difficult it had been to clean the mirrors, she asked him to show the girls how much effort was required.

He took out a long-handled squeegee, dipped it in the toilet and cleaned the mirror. Since then, there have been no lip prints on the mirror.

Words to Live By

Children, obey your parents in the Lord, for this is right.
Honor your father and mother (which is the first commandment
with a promise),
so that it may be well with you and that you may
live long on the earth.

EPHESIANS 6:1-3

Just Some Ideas

My grandmother died in 1997, and my family flew out to
Florida for the funeral. It was the first time I'd seen all my uncles
and cousins at the same time. My dad's side of the family had
their share of problems, so there might have been a little tension
in the air.

I remember noticing a guy with a beard walking toward the
gravesite. He looked like a homeless person wandering around,
so I didn't pay much attention. As he got closer, some of my relatives started to cry and tell everyone, "It's David! It's David!"
Then I recognized him. It was my cousin David Praytor, whom
no one had seen for 10 years.

Apparently he had run away from home when he was 16,
got hooked on drugs and had been wandering the streets of
Pensacola ever since. He told us that he had just happened to
look in the paper that morning and seen that Mercedes Praytor
had died and that the funeral was that day. So he came.

I tell you that story because of the talk I had with David at
the end of the funeral. (I had spent a summer with him when I
was a kid, so seeing him was a bittersweet experience.) He pulled
me aside and said, "Richard, don't turn out like me. Finish
school, work hard and, please, obey your parents. They want the

best for you and that's why they discipline you. Don't be like me. Listen to what others have to say. Make something of your life."

And with that, he waved to everyone and walked away.

Believe it or not, your parents want the best for you. They want you to succeed and make it in life on your own. They've been through life, so they know what mistakes to avoid and want to pass along the wisdom they've learned along the way. Don't try to fight your parents; it will only make things worse. You know it's true.

Do you find it difficult to obey your parents? Ask God to give you the strength to obey them because that's what He has commanded. One day, sooner or later, you'll obey them because you want to, not because you have to.

Prayer

I ask for strength, Lord, strength to obey the
people who provide for me,
who give me a home and love me.
I pray that I will respect and honor them
as You have called us to do.
I also pray that I would be a good mother/
father to my kids,
leading them to know and love You.
Amen.

33

HUMILITY

Some people wear their halos too tight.

A friend just got back from a holiday skiing trip to Utah with the kind of story that warms the cockles of anybody's heart. Conditions were perfect: 12 degrees below, no feeling in the toes, basic numbness all over, the "tell me when we're having fun" kind of day.

One of the women in the group complained to her husband that she was in dire need of a restroom. He told her not to worry, that he was sure there was relief waiting at the top of the lift in the form of a powder room for female skiers in distress. He was wrong, of course, and the pain did not go away. If you've ever had nature hit its panic button in you, then you know that a temperature of 12 degrees below doesn't help matters.

So with time running out, the woman weighed her options. Her husband, picking up on the intensity of the pain, suggested that since she was wearing an all-white ski outfit, she should go off into the woods and no one would even notice (the white would provide more than adequate camouflage). So she headed for the tree line, began lowering her ski pants and proceeded to do her thing. If you've ever parked on the side of a slope, then you know there is a right way and wrong way to set your skis so that you don't move.

Yup, you got it! She had them positioned the wrong way. Steep slopes are not forgiving, even during the most embarrassing moments. Without warning, the woman found herself skiing backward, out-of-control, racing through the trees (somehow missing all of them) and onto another slope. Her derriere and the reverse side were still bare, her pants were down around her knees, and she was picking up speed all the while.

She continued backward, totally out-of-control, creating an unusual sideshow for the other skiers. The woman slid back under the lift and finally collided violently with a pylon. The bad news was that she broke her arm and was unable to pull up her ski pants. At long last her husband arrived, put an end to her nudie show and then summoned the ski patrol. They transported her to a hospital.

While in the emergency room, a man with an obviously broken leg was put in the bed next to hers.

"So, how'd you break your leg?" she asked, making small talk.

"It was the darnedest thing you ever saw," he said. "I was riding up this ski lift and suddenly I couldn't believe my eyes. There was this crazy woman skiing backward out-of-control, down the mountain, with her bare bottom hanging out of her clothes and her pants down around her knees. I leaned over to get a better look and fell out of the lift . . . So, how'd you break your arm?"

Words to Live By

But He gives a greater grace.
Therefore it says,
"God is opposed to the proud,
but gives grace to the humble."

JAMES 4:6

Just Some Ideas

Do you ever get too big for your britches and then get humbled by the Guy upstairs? Yeah, me too. Once I performed with a buddy of mine during a chapel service at a Christian school. After chapel was over, the kids ran up to us wanting to get our autographs and have pictures taken with us. We literally were there for a half-hour, signing Bibles, notebooks and T-shirts for these kids. Talk about being on cloud nine—we were strutting like two semi-famous Christian celebrities.

As we walked to the parking lot, all the kids were lined up by the school waving good-bye to us. When we got to my friend's car, the kids saw that it was a red 1994 Saturn that hadn't been washed in several months. One kid yelled out, "Hey, nice car, funny guys." All the kids started laughing as we got into the car and drove off. That brought us back to reality.

Humility is always a virtue that's "in style." People will always notice it and tell others about it. Along with humility come good rapport, likeability and free cuts in line. When you're humble, people tend to not talk bad about you because if they did, they look like the jerk. Humble people are sure of themselves, which translates into a better witness for Christ.

Have you ever met one of those people who is so cocky that it just makes you laugh? It's the opposite with humility. People appreciate those who can put others before themselves.

Are you a humble person? Do you routinely put yourself or others first in line? The Bible says we need to be humble. Why? Because humility will take you farther in life than anything else. (Well, maybe an ice cold frappuccino will take you farther.)

Ask God for humility in every facet of your life and, I guarantee, you'll be lifted up higher than you ever thought possible.

Prayer

I pray for humility in my life.
Show me ways to humble myself at home, at work,
in the company of strangers.
Convict me when I become proud
and remind me to be Christlike so that I can
be a better witness for You.
Amen.

DRAWING CLOSE TO GOD

*Most of us spend the first six days of each week sowing wild oats,
then we go to church on Sunday and pray for crop failure.*
FRED ALLEN

A man in Topeka, Kansas, decided to write a book about churches around the country. He started by flying to San Francisco and
started working east from there. Going to a very large church, he
began taking photographs and making notes. He spotted a gold-
en telephone on the vestibule wall and was intrigued with a sign
that read "$10,000 a minute."

Seeking out the pastor, he asked about the phone and the
sign. The pastor answered that this golden phone was, in fact,
a direct line to heaven and if he paid the price, he could talk
directly to God.

The man thanked the pastor and continued on his way.
As he continued to visit churches in Seattle, Salt Lake, Denver,
Chicago, Milwaukee and around the rest of the United States,
he found more phones, with the same sign, and the same answer
from each pastor.

Finally, he arrived in Amarillo, Texas. Upon entering a
church, behold, he saw the usual golden telephone. But *this*
time, the sign read "Calls: 25 cents each." Fascinated, he asked
to talk to the pastor.

"Reverend, I have been in cities all across the country, and
in each church I have found this golden telephone and have
been told it is a direct line to heaven, but in the other churches

the cost was $10,000 a minute. Your sign says it's just 25 cents a call. Why?"

The pastor, smiling benignly, replied, "Son, you're in Texas now. It's a local call."

Words to Live By

Make me know Your ways, O LORD; teach me Your paths.
Lead me in Your truth and teach me,
for You are the God of my salvation;
for You I wait all the day.

PSALM 25:4-5

Just Some Ideas

If you want to get close to God, watch the movie *The Omen*. That flick will definitely have you saying your prayers tonight. It's about the devil's child being born in preparation for the end of the world. (I'm pretty sure that child lives down my street because there's a kid who lives a few houses down from me who is always causing trouble.) Anyway, after watching the movie, I felt a little uneasy and didn't want any nightmares, so I prayed. It seems the majority of people want to start—or renew—their relationship with God when something bad happens or when they're about to take a final exam.

So what does being close to God mean? Going to church more? Tithing more? Being a Republican? Well, it could mean *any* of these things, but *none* of them necessarily implies a relationship with God. There are a number of things we can do to get closer to the Almighty, but they're different for each person. For some people, it's being alone and praying. For others, it's going to a place with tons of people and worshiping as the Body of Christ.

For me, being close to God means going fishing. About 30 miles from my house, there's a lake in the middle of a beautiful woods—and there's hardly ever anyone there. I sit there on the shore with my line in the water, daydreaming of what it's like in heaven. I think about what I'll say to God when I see Him. I think about what He'll say to me when He finds out I met my wife on the Internet. You know, we'll talk about serious stuff like that.

It's so neat to think that the incredible God of the universe, the Supreme Being who is so far beyond time and space, would love to sit with you one day and watch the World Series of Poker on ESPN. That's how much He loves you. And it doesn't matter how far you run away; it always takes only one step to get back to Him.

So how do you get close to God? Start off by just talking to Him. Whether you do it on your knees before you go to bed or when there's a cop behind you on the freeway, talk to God. Then pick up that book you carry to church under your arm— you know, the one that never gets opened. Read a chapter, a paragraph or even just a verse. And once in a while, buy some lunch for the guy who sits by the freeway exit holding up a cardboard sign asking for money. Little things like that will draw you closer to God than any *Touched by an Angel* episode ever will.

Prayer

Father, teach me how to draw close to You.
Take away any distractions in my life
that get in the way of my relationship with You.
Show me how to be a better follower of You,
and fill my heart with Your presence.
Amen.

POINTING OUT FAULTS

You can't keep blaming yourself.
Just blame yourself once and move on.
HOMER SIMPSON

A wife was making a breakfast of fried eggs for her husband. Suddenly her husband burst into the kitchen. "Careful . . . *Careful!* Put in some more butter! Oh, my *gosh!* You're cooking too many at once. *Too many!* Turn them! *Turn them now!* We need more butter. Oh, my *gosh! Where* are we going to get *more butter*? They're going to *stick!* Careful . . . *Careful!* I said be *careful!* You *never* listen to me when you're cooking! Never! Turn them! Hurry up! Are you *crazy?* Have you *lost* your mind? Don't forget to salt them. You know you always forget to salt them. Use the salt. *Use the salt! The salt!*"

The wife stared at him. "What in the world is wrong with you? You think I don't know how to fry a couple of eggs?"

The husband calmly replied, "I wanted to show you what it feels like when I'm driving with you in the car."

Words to Live By

Why do you look at the speck that is in your brother's eye,
but do not notice the log that is in your own eye?
Or how can you say to your brother,
"Let me take the speck out of your eye," and behold,
the log in your own eye?

You hypocrite, first take the log out of your own eye,
and then you will see clearly to take the speck
out of your brother's eye.

MATTHEW 7:3-5, *NIV*

Just Some Ideas

I was watching *The Apprentice* last night—you know, the show where at the end of every episode, they fire someone, until only one person is left at the end. This past episode, Donald Trump asked one particular woman why her team didn't win the contest. She started to blame everyone else on the team, and immediately Mr. Trump said, "You're blaming everyone else but yourself. You're fired!"

As I shoved the last cheese-dipped tortilla chip into my mouth, I thought to myself, *Does Mr. Trump comb his hair like that on purpose? For being a billionaire, Donald Trump has a $3 haircut.*

But back to our story. When you point out someone else's faults, you end up looking like a jerk. Even if you're completely right and it's all true, you're the jerk. I don't know why that is. I guess it all goes back to Adam and Eve. Eve ate the forbidden fruit and when Adam blamed Eve, he got in trouble. Not much has changed today.

So what do you do when someone screws up and you have the opportunity to say something? Here's what you should do: Shut up. Believe me, God will deal with that person in His own way and in His own time. If you choose to walk away from a situation like that, good things will happen. First, you won't be the jerk. Second, people will take notice that you're a good and decent person. And third, the person in question will respect and appreciate you a ton since you didn't make him or her look bad (and you'll probably get a free lunch).

We live in a society that encourages people to blame others. It's all about a "looking out for number one" mentality. But remember, the second greatest commandment is to love our neighbors and treat them the way we'd like to be treated.

So the next time your coworker messes up on his TPS reports, just let it go . . . and go back to playing solitaire.

Prayer

Thank You, God, for not pointing out every
bad thing I've ever done.
You are perfect and yet You've never bragged about it.
Teach me to be humble.
Show me when to swallow my pride and when
to keep my mouth shut.
And most of all, thank You for loving a sinner like me.
Amen.

CULTURALLY RELEVANT

*An anthropologist has just come back from a
field trip to New Guinea
with reports of a tribe so primitive that they have Tide
but not new Tide with lemon fresh Borax.*
DAVID LETTERMAN

One day while they were bungee jumping, Oley said to Sven, "You know, we could make a lot of money running our own bungee-jumping service in Mexico." Sven thought it was a great idea, and so they pooled their money and bought everything they'd need: a tower, an elastic cord, insurance, and so on. They traveled to Mexico and began to set up their equipment in the town square.

As they constructed the tower, a crowd began to assemble. Slowly, more and more people gathered to watch them at work. When the tower was finished, the crowd was so large that Oley and Sven thought it would be smart to give a demonstration.

They climbed the tower together. Oley strapped Sven into the harness—and Sven jumped. Sven bounced at the end of the cord, but when he came back up, Oley noticed he had a few cuts and scratches. Unfortunately, Oley couldn't grab him before he fell again. When Sven came back up again, he was bruised and bleeding. Again, Oley failed to catch him. Sven went down again and bounced back up. By the time Oley caught him, Sven was nearly unconscious, with a couple of broken bones. Alarmed, Oley asked, "What happened?! Sven, are you okay?! Was the cord too long?"

Barely able to speak, Sven gasped, "No, the bungee cord was fine. It was the crowd . . . What the heck is a piñata?"

Words to Live By

And He spoke many things to them in parables, saying:
"The sower went out to sow, and as he sowed,
some seeds fell beside the road, and the birds came and ate them up.
Others fell on the rocky places, where they did not have much soil;
and immediately they sprang up, because they had no depth of soil.
But when the sun had risen, they were scorched;
and because they had no root, they withered away.
Others fell among the thorns, and the thorns came
up and choked them out.
And others fell on the good soil and yielded a crop,
some a hundredfold, some sixty, and some thirty.

MATTHEW 13:3-8

Just Some Ideas

The Passion of the Christ by Mel Gibson has become the number one R-rated movie of all time. It is also the only movie that made me not want to eat my popcorn or drink my soda. (That saved me about $55 dollars, not including the price of the movie.)

I read a Hollywood movie critic's review of the film, in which he stated that it was too violent. Please tell me that critic was smoking a joint that morning. He was saying that a film about Jesus was too violent, but other films are okay? Sure, movies such as *Scream, Freddy vs. Jason, The Exorcist IV* and *Van Helsing* are the ones you should bring your children to see on Christmas Eve.

Yes, *The Passion of the Christ* was violent, but it was reality. If Gibson had made a Jesus movie that attempted to downplay the reality of Christ's suffering, it would have been a flop. No one wants to see a corny Jesus movie, especially someone who is not a Christian.

Not only did Gibson choose to go violent with the movie, but he also chose a leading Hollywood star to play the part of Jesus. He chose someone who could actually act, not a person who was friends with the producer's assistant's niece who knew this guy who hadn't shaved in a couple of years and looked like Jesus. Gibson knew that he had to be culturally relevant to make an impact on nonbelievers.

That's why I love visiting churches where pastors are not afraid to joke around and be bold in their sermons. I appreciate pastors who don't try to impress the congregation with their knowledge of the Bible but who convey the reality of God in our lives in a way anyone can understand. God wants us to be cool, not square.

Prayer

*Father, I pray that I will impact my community
in a relevant way.
Please lead me not into cheesiness but into a path
where I can show others
that You are a cool and fun God.
And thank You for not making us wear plaid.
Amen.*

DON'T BE DUMB

Stupidity is ignorance multiplied by cable television.
RICH PRAYTOR

Got a letter from Grandma the other day. She wrote:

The other day, I went up to a local Christian book-store and saw a "Honk If You Love Jesus" bumper stick-er. I was feeling particularly sassy that day, because I had just come from a thrilling choir performance, fol-lowed by a thunderous prayer meeting, so I bought the sticker and put it on my bumper. Boy, I'm glad I did! What an uplifting experience followed!

I was stopped at a red light at a busy intersection, just lost in thought about the Lord and how good He is . . . and I didn't notice that the light had changed. It is a good thing someone else loves Jesus, because if he hadn't honked, I'd never have noticed! I found that *lots* of people love Jesus!

Why, while I was sitting there, the guy behind me started honking like crazy, and then he leaned out of his window and screamed, "For the love of *God*! *Go*! *Go*! *Jesus Christ, go!*"

What an exuberant cheerleader he was for Jesus! Everyone started honking! I just leaned out of my win-dow and started waving and smiling at all these loving people. I even honked my horn a few times to share in the love!

I saw another guy waving in a funny way with only his middle finger stuck up in the air. When I asked my teenaged grandson in the back seat what that meant, he said that it was probably a Hawaiian greeting.

Well, I've never met anyone from Hawaii before, so I leaned out the window and returned the loving greeting. My grandson burst out laughing . . . why even he was enjoying this religious experience! A couple of the people were so caught up in the joy of the moment that they got out of their cars and started walking toward me. I bet they wanted to pray or ask what church I attended, but this is when I noticed the light had changed.

So, I waved to all my sisters and brothers, grinning, and drove on through the intersection. I noticed I was the only car that got through the intersection before the light changed again, and I felt kind of sad that I had to leave them after all the love we had shared. So I slowed the car down, leaned out the window and gave them all the Hawaiian greeting one last time as I drove away. Praise the Lord for such wonderful folks!

Grandma

Words to Live By

The heart of the wise instructs his mouth, and adds persuasiveness to his lips.

PROVERBS 16:23

Just Some Ideas

I don't like dumb people. They annoy me.

When I say "dumb," I mean people who choose to ignore things around them and are not considerate. An example of a dumb person would be someone who merges into my lane while I'm in it. That's grounds for having your left arm hacked off (remember, if I get hacked, you're getting hacked).

I watched the movie *Envy* the other day with my wife. It stars Jack Black and Ben Stiller, who are both great actors. Yet the movie was terrible. I was actually dumber after watching it—and afterward I had to go read a dictionary to bring my IQ back up.

The movie was about two hardworking guys who were best friends. One of them becomes rich and the other gets extremely jealous. In the end, they become friends again. That's it. That's the movie. Dumb, dumb, stupid.

I find a lot of so-called Christians are spiritually dumb. They profess their faith in Christ and yet act like morons. They gossip, cheat on their taxes or watch *Baywatch* in their underwear. If you call yourself a Christian, don't act like one—live like one.

One of my biggest pet peeves is when a group of church folks go to a restaurant and leave a religious track as a tip. They think leaving a piece of paper that says, "You're a sinner and probably going to hell" is a great way to tell someone about God. Think again, freak!

How about leaving a couple of dollars more than you really need to? What a blessing it would be for that waiter or waitress. Instead of thinking of you as a psycho, cheap Christian, they'll want to serve you again. Remember WWJT—What Would Jesus Tip?

Prayer

*Father, give me wisdom and prevent me from
ever being spiritually dumb.
I pray that I would be aware of my actions
whether I'm around people or alone.
Thank You, God, for giving me wisdom—
I pray I would use it often.
Amen*

GOOD CREDIT

*If you think nobody cares whether you're alive or dead,
try missing a couple of car payments.*
ANN LANDERS

When the preacher's car broke down on a country road, he walked to a nearby roadhouse to use the phone. After calling for a tow truck, he spotted his old friend Frank, drunk and shabbily dressed at the bar. "What happened to you, Frank?" asked the good reverend. "You used to be rich."

Frank told a sad tale of bad investments that had led to his downfall. How after the divorce, his wife took everything. Then he got involved with some shady businessmen who took the rest of his money. With the last pennies he had to his name, he gambled them away.

"Go home," the preacher said. "Open your Bible at random, stick your finger on the page and there will be God's answer."

Some time later, the preacher bumped into Frank, who was wearing Gucci shoes, sporting a Rolex watch and had just stepped out of a Mercedes. "Frank," said the preacher, "I am glad to see things really turned around for you."

"Yes, preacher, and I owe it all to you," said Frank. "I opened my Bible, put my finger down on the page and there was the answer . . . Chapter 11."

Words to Live By

Then the lord of that slave felt compassion and released him
and forgave him the debt.

MATTHEW 18:27

Just Some Ideas

It's amazing how much debt Americans are in today. I lived on Top Ramen for a couple of years because my credit card debt was so high. My whole paycheck was going toward paying the minimum amount on my cards, and I was still broke. I seriously thought about filing bankruptcy, but I couldn't afford to pay the legal fees. I wanted to say, "Can I put it on my card?" Luckily, I inherited an RV, which I then sold and was able to pay off everything. But many people are not as fortunate as I was.

Debt can be terribly demoralizing. You worry constantly about making the payment on time or if there's going to be enough money for rent. Once you have a late payment on your record, your whole credit history is down the toilet. Your house is more expensive, trying to buy a car is a hassle and your mother-in-law tells your wife, "I told you so!"

So what do you do if you're deep in debt? Well, it depends on where you are in life. If you're young and have a ton of debt, call and make arrangements with your creditors. Ask them to lower the interest rate or get on a payment plan. They would rather have their money later than not at all. Make sure you pay your rent and car payment. There are so many different programs now that will still allow you to buy a home or get another credit card as you pay off your old debt.

If you're older, determine whether you'll be moving in the next several years. If so, you might want to try to pay off everything.

If not, then start over. Why? Because unless you're making a bunch of money and can pay off your debt with all the interest, there's no use in suffering. Credit card companies and their interest rates are almost criminal. There's no way to pay off your debt by paying the minimum payment.

Don't get me wrong—I'm not at all encouraging people to be irresponsible or to run away from their debt. I think everyone should try to pay it off, but when it's taking food off your table or hindering your quality of life, then you should take action.

Prayer

Father, I pray that I would be wise with my finances.
I pray I would find ways to get out of any debt
that I might have and come up with a financial plan
that is pleasing to You. Thank You for money and the
blessing it can be when used wisely.
Amen.

THE RULES—THIS TIME BY MEN

A man will pay $2 for a $1 item he needs.
A woman will pay $1 for a $2 item that she doesn't
need but is on sale.

We always hear "The Rules" from the female perspective. Now here are The Rules from the male side of life:

1. Learn to work the toilet seat. You're a big girl. If it's up, put it down. We need it up, you need it down. You don't hear us complaining about your leaving it down.

2. Sometimes we are not thinking about you. Live with it.

3. Sunday = sports. It's like the full moon or the changing of the tides. Let it be.

4. Shopping is *not* a sport. And no, we are never going to think of it that way.

5. Crying is blackmail.

6. Ask for what you want. Let us be clear on this one: Subtle hints do not work! Strong hints do not work! Obvious hints do not work! Just say it!

7. We don't remember dates. Mark birthdays and anniversaries on a calendar. Remind us frequently beforehand.

8. Most guys own three pairs of shoes—tops. What makes you think we'd be any good at choosing which pair, out of 30, would look good with your dress?

9. "Yes" and "no" are perfectly acceptable answers to almost every question.

10. Come to us with a problem only if you want help solving it. That's what we do. Sympathy is what your girlfriends are for.

11. A headache that lasts for 17 months is a problem. See a doctor.

12. Check your oil! Please.

13. Anything we said six months ago is inadmissible in an argument. In fact, all comments become null and void after seven days.

14. If you think you're fat, you probably are. Don't ask us. We refuse to answer.

15. If something we said can be interpreted two ways, and one of the ways makes you sad or angry, we meant the other one.

16. Whenever possible, please say whatever you have to say during commercials.

17. Christopher Columbus did not need directions, and neither do we.

18. The relationship is never going to be like it was the first two months we were going out. Get over it. And quit whining to your girlfriends.

19. *All* men see in only 16 colors, like a Windows default setting. Peach, for example, is a fruit, not a color. Pumpkin is also a fruit. We have no idea what mauve is.

20. We are not mind readers and we never will be. Our lack of mind-reading ability is not proof of how little we care about you.

21. If we ask what is wrong and you say "nothing," we will act like nothing's wrong. We know you are lying, but it is just not worth the hassle.

22. If you ask a question you don't want an answer to, expect an answer you don't want to hear.

23. When we have to go somewhere, absolutely anything you wear is fine. Really.

24. You have enough clothes. You have too many shoes.

25. I'm in shape. *Round* is a shape.

26. Thank you for reading this. Yes, I know, I have to sleep on the couch tonight, but did you know we really don't mind that? It's like camping.

Words to Live By

*For this reason a man shall leave his father and mother
and shall be joined to his wife, and the two shall become one flesh.*

EPHESIANS 5:31

Just Some Ideas

When I first started writing this book, I was single. I thought I knew it all. Now I'm married and realize that I don't know a single thing about women. All I know is that they get upset when you use the drapes as a towel.

I'm lucky, though, because my wife is the most low-maintenance woman I've ever met. She's 6' 1", so buying clothes consists of going online and ordering specially made pants and shirts. She's very athletic and doesn't like to wear jewelry, so that eliminates the horrific nightmare of buying her diamonds and rubies. Her favorite thing to do is to stay home with friends and family and play board games. Yes, folks, I'm very blessed.

Although my wife is near perfect, we still have our moments. For instance, my wife is a bed hog. We have a king-size bed, yet my area to sleep is only about 17 inches wide. To top it off, she'll pull over all the covers and leave me to face the cold, dark night in only my Superman boxers (yes, I have cartoon boxers).

Another thing we deal with is climate control. If the temperature of the room drops below 87 degrees, she gets cold. My wife starts to shiver while I'm sweating profusely, clinging to any available oxygen left in the area. I'm not sure what God was thinking when He made women, but I think His intention was to keep all husbands humble.

So what's my point? To be honest, I don't have one. I simply want to convey that women and men are different. Marriage is the ultimate institution in which these differences are brought together to create happiness. I love my wife more than anything, which means I love the ways in which she and I are different. Because of our differences, we are growing together. Even though she takes up 87 percent of the bed and keeps the covers for herself, I know she's only a tug away. I like that better than waking up alone every morning (except when we've had Mexican food for dinner).

Prayer

Father, give me the grace
to accept the ways in which other people
are different from me.
I pray I would embrace the differences I have
with my spouse
and learn to accept them as he/she accepts mine.
Thank You, God, for differences
and the joy they bring.
Amen.

FORGIVENESS

It's easier to ask for forgiveness than for permission.
RICH PRAYTOR

As a woman was walking along the beach, she saw a bottle in the sand. She picked it up and pulled out the cork. Whoosh! A big puff of smoke appeared.

"You have released me from my prison," the genie told her. "To show my thanks, I grant you three wishes. But take care, for with each, your husband will receive double of whatever you request."

"Why?" the woman asked. "That bum left me for another woman."

"That is how it is written," replied the genie.

The woman shrugged and then asked for $1 million. There was a flash of light, and $1 million appeared at her feet. At the same instant, in a far-off place, her wayward husband looked down to see twice that amount at his feet.

"And your second wish?"

"Genie, I want the world's most expensive diamond necklace."

Another flash of light, and the woman was holding the precious treasure.

And in that distant place, her husband was looking for a gem broker to buy his latest bonanza.

"Genie, is it really true that my husband has $2 million and more jewels than I do, and that he gets double of whatever I wish for?"

The genie said it was indeed true.

"Okay, genie, I'm ready for my last wish," the woman said. "Scare me half to death."

Words to Live By

Therefore, let it be known to you, brethren,
that through Him forgiveness of sins is proclaimed to you.

ACTS 13:38

Just Some Ideas

About four years ago a close friend of mine went behind my back and booked a show I had been trying to get for a while. I was furious. I was so upset I couldn't see straight. I thought of every conceivable thing I could do and say to this person. I even thought about showing up at the event and embarrassing us both. But in the end I did the Christian thing . . . I spread rumors about him.

Actually, I ended up letting go of the situation and forgetting it ever happened (until now). I realized that it didn't matter how angry I got; it wasn't going to change the situation.

People will always let you down. Your best friend, your wife, your pastor and even Jack Bauer will never measure up to your standards all the time. The thing we must realize is that God has forgiven us, and in turn, we should forgive others. How fair is it that God wipes our slate clean, yet we get upset when someone else screws up?

In the New Testament we hear about an adulterous woman who is dragged out into the street by an angry mob and is about to be stoned. Then Jesus steps in front of the crowd and says, "He who is without sin, cast the first stone." Everyone walks

away. I like that story because it teaches us that God is so forgiving that He'll rescue us when an angry mob is about to get us.
(An angry mob, in my case, is a family reunion.)

As you leave your house today to do the things that you do,
remember the fine art of forgiving. When your coworker
reports to your boss that you've been playing too much solitaire at work, let it go. If someone cuts you off on the freeway,
let it go. Or if your spouse spends an astronomical amount of
money on a worthless item, throw cold water on your spouse
while he or she is showering. And then let it go.

Prayer

Father, give me a forgiving heart.
Let me forget all the bad things people have done
to me and my family.
I pray I would let things go as soon as they happen
and that I would forgive as quickly as You do.
Amen.

41

POLITICS

Politics is the art of looking for trouble, finding it everywhere, diagnosing it incorrectly and applying the wrong remedy.
GROUCHO MARX

A Republican and a Democrat are seated next to each other on a flight from Los Angeles to New York. The Democrat asks the Republican if he'd like to play a fun game. The Republican, tired, just wants to take a nap, so he politely declines and rolls over to the window to catch a few winks. The Democrat persists and explains that the game is easy and a lot of fun.

He says, "I ask you a question, and if you don't know the answer, you pay me $5, and vice versa."

Again, the Republican declines and tries to get some sleep.

The Democrat, now agitated, says, "Okay, if you don't know the answer, you pay me $5, and if I don't know the answer, I will pay you $500."

This catches the Republican's attention, and figuring there will be no end to this torment unless he plays, he agrees to the game.

The Democrat asks the first question: "What's the distance from Earth to the moon?" The Republican doesn't say a word, reaches into his wallet, pulls out a $5 bill and hands it to the Democrat.

"Okay," says the Democrat, "your turn."

The Republican asks, "What goes up a hill with three legs and comes down with four legs?"

The Democrat, puzzled, takes out his laptop computer and searches all his references—no answer. He taps into the air phone with his modem and searches the Internet and the Library of Congress—no answer.

Frustrated, he sends e-mails to all his friends and coworkers but to no avail.

After an hour, he wakes the Republican and hands him $500. The Republican thanks him and turns back to get some more sleep.

The Democrat, who is more than a little miffed, stirs the Republican and asks, "Well, what's the answer?"

Without a word, the Republican reaches into his wallet, hands the Democrat $5 and goes back to sleep.

Words to Live By

And He said to them, "Whose likeness and inscription is this?"
They said to Him, "Caesar's."
Then He said to them, "Then render to Caesar the things
that are Caesar's,
and to God the things that are God's."

MATTHEW 22:20-21

Just Some Ideas

Here's a subject I know very little about, but I'm going to write about it anyway. (I sound like a politician.) I never really kept up on some of the things going on in D.C. until the last presidential election. I actually watched the debates on television with my wife and enjoyed it—I know, that means I'm getting old. But I realized something as we watched the second debate. The candidates never answer the question that is asked. They shoot off on some tangent where no human has gone before. The commentator will ask, "Sir, if elected, are you going to raise taxes?" The candidate answers, "Well, the question really focuses on the Alaskan pipeline where the peninsula meets the region adjacent to the area where the most caribou will be affected in the summer months." I'm sitting there thinking, *Did he call my mom a caribou?*

Politicians and the rest of the population who avoid direct questions with flimsy answers are not usually looked up to. This happened a lot at my old job. Our supervisor would ask an employee about a client's complaint and get a 10-minute "it's not my fault" reply. The supervisor would say, "I wasn't accusing you of anything—I just want to know the facts."

The measure of a person, I believe, is how honest and straightforward he or she is. My buddy Nazareth is an honest and very straightforward person. When I ask him his thoughts on something, he gives it to me straight, whether I like the answer or not. But because of that, I've grown a lot faster in my career than I would have had I listened to someone who just blows smoke up my you-know-what (and believe me, you don't want smoke up there).

In your daily life, think about how much you tend to avoid being honest out of convenience or because it's quicker to be dishonest. Make it a point to really think about an answer to someone's question. Ask yourself, *Am I being truthful? Is it okay to voice my honest opinion? How long will my wife make me sleep on the couch?*

God calls us to be honest people, even when it's going to tick someone off. Ask God for guidance and help to be a more genuine person. When we do this, our conscience begins to clear and our relationship with Him will be that much sweeter. (Plus, you'll be a certified Republican.)

Prayer

*Father, I pray that I would live a life
of honesty, integrity, straightforwardness and courage.
Mold me into a person You can be proud of.
I pray I will never hide behind excuses
and that my character will never be compromised.
Amen.*

42

COMPUTERS

In the computer revolution,
everything changes way too fast for the human brain to comprehend.
That is why only 14 year olds really understand what is going on.
DAVE BARRY

Shortly after Bill Gates was killed in a freak accident, he found himself being sized up by St. Peter. "Bill, this is a tough call. You've made great technological advancements with Microsoft, but you've also given us Windows 95. I think I'm going to let you choose between heaven and hell."

"That sounds fair," Gates replied. "May I have a look at hell first?"

And so first St. Peter took him to hell.

"This is hell? Wow, look at all those gorgeous women, the ones that laughed when I asked them out on dates in high school. And look at those mansions!" exclaimed Bill.

"And see all those coders?" Peter pointed out. "They work 24 hours a day for free just because they really love you, Bill, and live only to please you."

"Shazam, this is all virtual, isn't it, St. Peter?"

"Yep. With no bugs, Bill."

"If this is hell, what can heaven be like?"

St. Peter made a sweeping gesture and replied, "Like this!"

"People wearing robes and playing harps while they sit on clouds? What a boring cliché. I'll take hell!" replied Gates.

And so two weeks later, St. Peter paid Bill a little visit.

"Hey, what's going on? It's nearly 200 degrees and the air is terrible. There's no food or drink. Goblins jab me in the ribs constantly. I'm crawling with vermin and weak with disease. They play the Beastie Boys at all hours, for all eternity. There are *no computers*! Where are the women, the program slaves, the virtual wonders? Where is the splendid hell you promised me?" cried Gates.

"Oh, that—that was just a demo . . ."

Words to Live By

And this I pray,
that your love may abound
still more and more in
real knowledge and all discernment,
so that you may approve the things
that are excellent,
in order to be sincere and blameless
until the day of Christ.

PHILIPPIANS 1:9-10

Just Some Ideas

I remember back when I was in school, if you liked a girl, you would write her a note saying, "If you want to be my girlfriend, check box A. If you don't, check box B." Now today with technology, things are completely different. If a boy wants to ask out a girl, he e-mails her saying, "If you want to be my girl, double click here. If you don't, then download this attachment."

Times are definitely changing. When I first started doing comedy, I wrote everything down in notebooks or on restaurant napkins. Now, I have a database of jokes saved on both of my computers. Computers are great if you use them wisely. Most of us use them to access the Internet, where you can buy, find, sell or marry anything imaginable.

Then you have the Internet garbage—you know what I'm talking about. This garbage has ruined many lives and will continue to do so if something is not done. This issue is not really addressed publicly in the church because it causes so much embarrassment. But if it's not dealt with openly, people won't know how to deal with it.

So I've come up with some safeguards we can all use if we have the Internet at home. Well, I didn't really come up with them—I'm just putting the really good ones I've found together in a list, but anyway . . .

- **Safeguard #1.** Put your computer in a high traffic area of the house, like the living room or the den. This will prevent your being tempted to surf on sites that aren't approved by Grandma.

- **Safeguard #2.** Download a program that filters adult content. The best one out there is www.besafe.com. It doesn't allow any adult sites to be on your computer, even if you have the password to unlock the program.

- **Safeguard #3.** Put a big ol' picture of Jesus right above the computer. You'll feel guilty just sitting down.

Technology is a wonderful thing, but sometimes you've got to go back to the old-school way of doing things and kick the devil between the legs.

Prayer

Father, I pray for purity of my mind,
my heart and my spirit.
Cleanse my mind and restore the innocence
I use to have.
You make all things new. Make me new.
Make my mind new and lead me not into
temptation but deliver me from evil.
Amen.

Well, if you're reading this, it means you're finished with the book or are cheating and skipping to the end. Either way, thank you for being a part of a project that has been on my heart for many years. I wanted to write something believers could enjoy and through which they could learn about God. I also wanted to write something that people who normally don't go to church could enjoy that would give them a deeper understanding of what Christianity is all about.

I believe humor is one of the most powerful ways to convey the message of the gospel. If you've ever seen mainstream comedians on TV, they make you laugh and *then* tell you that they're gay. You see, it's easier to tell someone something deep about yourself after you've made him or her laugh and have connected with him or her on some sort of level. When you disguise sin with humor, it's much easier to accept.

So let's take back humor for what it was originally made for: to reach people for Christ. I believe Jesus had a great sense of humor when He walked the earth. I think when He was hanging out with the disciples, He probably joked around with Peter and made everyone laugh from time to time. I bet God the Father, with all His glory up in heaven, told the angels, "Hey, look, guys. I made this creature and put it in Australia. I took a beaver and a duck and put them into a mixing bowl. This is what came out. I call it a platypus." God definitely has a sense of humor.

So apart from this book, how can we use humor effectively to bring people back to faith? One way is to bring more humor into the Church. A pastor who uses jokes and funny illustrations in his sermon on Sunday morning will attract more attendees. When you have a fun pastor, you have a fun church. I love going to churches where the pastor has a great sense of humor, because I know the church will be the same. When you have a pastor who preaches in a monotone and rarely smiles, it's going to attract the same type of people.

When I was a youth leader back in Texas, the only way I could keep the kids' attention during my teaching was to throw in jokes every few minutes. Sometimes it would be in the form of a video clip or some goofy prop I brought from home. But after each joke, I would make a point about the truth of the Bible. The kids responded and remembered what I had to say because I showered the sermon with laughter. Laughter is extremely powerful and effective in conveying the message of Jesus Christ.

For some reason, non-Christians view humor in the Church as cheesy and not funny. In a way, they're right. In the past, the term "Christian comedy" often meant that someone had puppets or used goofy teeth while they told jokes. In the last 10 years, however, a new breed of Christian comedians has surfaced that have brought creative and hilarious material to the stage without compromising the faith. Comedy (or anything else, for that matter) is a more effective witnessing tool when it's great, not cheesy.

Brian Regan is my all-time favorite comedian. He's not only hilariously funny but also works incredibly clean. He has developed a following across the United States that is nothing short of amazing. He can go to any city and sell out the local civic center. Why? Because he's a great comedian and has been great for so long. Yet if you ask someone on the street if they've ever heard of Brian Regan, they'll probably say no. He's never been in a movie or on a TV show (that I know of), but he still packs out venues every month. That's the power of being great at what you do. If we, as believers, determined to be great at what we do, we could be so much more effective for the cause of Christ.

Another way of using humor to reach the lost is to have a comedy concert at your church. Think about it. Instead of inviting someone to church, you invite him or her to watch a stand-up comedian at church. As I said before, laughter has incredible power for bringing people to Christ. At almost every show I perform, someone tells me that he or she brought a neighbor who didn't want to go to church but came to the show. That "bridging" event led to them becoming closer as friends until eventually that neighbor gave his or her life over to Christ. Who would have ever thought that humor could be used as an evangelism tool? God knew.

So how can you use this book to share your faith? Simple. Give it to someone as a gift. When I self-published this book several years ago, I sent a couple of copies to my mother. She was utterly amazed that I had written a book, as I barely made it through college. I went to visit her about six months later, and one of her friends came over who wasn't a churchgoer. As we began to talk, this woman shared with me that my mom had brought my book to her to read while she was in the hospital for her mastectomy. She said that she was nervous about the surgery, but when she starting reading the book, it made her laugh and set her at ease. She said she even said a little prayer while they wheeled her to the operating room. That's why I wrote this book. So someone could laugh and learn about the love of God.

Typically, when comedians are done with their show, they end on a laugh. So I thought I would here as well. This is a story I heard a couple of months ago that made me laugh until I had a hernia. It goes like this.

A guy buys a brand-new Lincoln Navigator for $42,500 with monthly payments of $560. Then he and a friend go duck hunting in upper Wisconsin.

Now, nothing good can happen when a story begins with "they go duck hunting in upper Wisconsin." It's midwinter and, of course, all of the lakes are frozen. These two guys go out on the ice with their guns, a black lab and, of course, the new Navigator. They decide they want to make a natural-looking open-water area for the ducks to focus on—something for the decoys to float on.

The two guys soon realize that making a hole in the ice large enough to invite a passing duck is going to take a little more power than the average drill auger or saw can produce. So they take a stick of dynamite with a short 40-second fuse out of the back of the new Navigator. Now these two rocket scientists, afraid that they might slip on the ice while trying to run away after lighting the fuse, decide to light the fuse and throw the stick of dynamite as far away as possible.

Remember the black lab? It had been trained to retrieve, especially things thrown by the owner. So the dog takes off across the ice at a high rate of speed and grabs the stick of dynamite, with the burning 40-second fuse, just as it hits the ice. The two men, now with soiled pants, start waving their arms and screaming so that the dog will stop. The dog, now apparently cheered on by his master, starts running back faster.

One hunter panics, grabs his shotgun and shoots the dog. The shotgun is loaded with number 8 birdshot—hardly enough to stop a black lab. The dog stops for a moment, slightly confused, and then continues toward them. The hunter shoots him again, and this time the dog becomes really confused and thinks that these two geniuses have gone insane. So the dog, still with the dynamite in its mouth, runs for cover underneath the brand-new Navigator.

Realizing what has happened, the men start screaming as they run for their low-IQ lives. Just then, the red-hot exhaust pipe on the truck touches the dog's rear end, which causes it to yelp, drop the dynamite under the truck and take off after its master.   The truck is blown to bits and sinks to the bottom of the lake, leaving our two heroes standing there with "I can't believe this just happened" looks on their faces.

When the guy who bought the Navigator returns home and files a claim, the insurance company says that sinking a vehicle in a lake by illegal use of explosives is not covered by the policy. And he still had yet to make the first of those $560-a-month payments.

The dog is okay and doing fine.

That's my time, folks. I'm here all week. Be sure to tip your waiters and waitresses.

TO CONTACT RICH PRAYTOR:

Rich Praytor Productions
P.O. Box 63441
Colorado Springs, CO 80962
866-356-7424

www.richpraytor.com
www.prank316.com

email: info@richpraytor.com

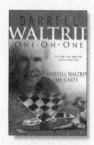